The MAILBOX® QUICK PLANS Math

grades 2-3

Group, Center, and Seatwork Activities

- Operations and algebraic thinking
- Number and operations in base ten
- Number and operations: fractions
- Measurement and data
- Geometry

30 key skills!

Managing Editor: Jennifer Bragg

Editorial Team: Becky S. Andrews, Debbie Ashworth, Diane Badden, Leann Baur, Michelle Bayless, Jacqueline Beaudry, Kimberley Bruck, Karen A. Brudnak, Pam Crane, Chris Curry, Colleen Dabney, Kathryn Davenport, David Drews, Barbara Duran, Ann Fisher, Kelli L. Gowdy, Karen Brewer Grossman, Tazmen Fisher Hansen, Marsha Heim, Lori Z. Henry, Troy Lawrence, April LoTempio, Andrea O'Donnell, Jennifer Otter, Beth Pallotta, Amy Payne, Kristin Priola, Mark Rainey, Cheryl Rayl, Greg D. Rieves, Kelly Robertson, Hope Rodgers-Medina, Amy Satkoski, Rebecca Saunders, Hope Taylor Spencer, Donna K. Teal, Sharon M. Tresino, Patricia Twohey, Teresa Vilfer-Snyder, Zane Williard, Virginia Zeletzki

www.themailbox.com

Table of Contents

COMMON CORE Aligned

www.themailbox.com/core

What's Inside

More than 150 activities on 30 key skills!

Two group activities

Two center activities

Patterns and more

One or more practice pages

Basic Facts

Group Work

● Draw a 3 x 6 grid on a vinyl shower curtain. Randomly program a grid space with a number from 1 to 9 so that each number is used two times. Invite a child to toss two beanbags onto the grid. If the beanbags land on the same grid space, have her toss one again. The student uses the numbers to state a math fact with a specified operation (addition or multiplication). If she is correct, she passes the beanbags to another student. If she is incorrect, help her state the fact correctly before passing the beanbags.

● Form teams of up to seven students. For each team, copy page 5 and program it with an operation and numbers as shown. Slip each paper in a plastic sheet protector (gameboard); then give a dry-erase marker and a gameboard to each team. To play, each team member takes a turn answering a problem or correcting a teammate's incorrect answer. The first team to correctly complete its gameboard wins.

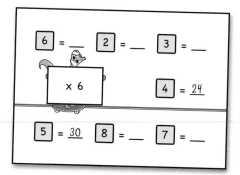

Centers

● Provide a container of plastic building bricks. A child chooses two bricks and counts the dots on each one; then he writes and solves a corresponding addition problem. He returns the bricks to the container and repeats the activity as time allows.

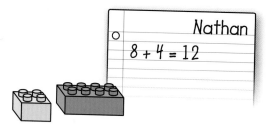

● *Partner Game:* Set out a laminated 4 x 4 grid, two different-colored wipe-off markers, and a set of basic fact flash cards. Player 1 takes a flash card and names the answer. If she is correct, she uses her marker to color a grid square. If she is incorrect, her turn ends. Alternate play continues until one student has colored four squares in a row.

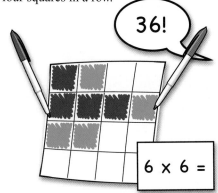

Seatwork See page 6.

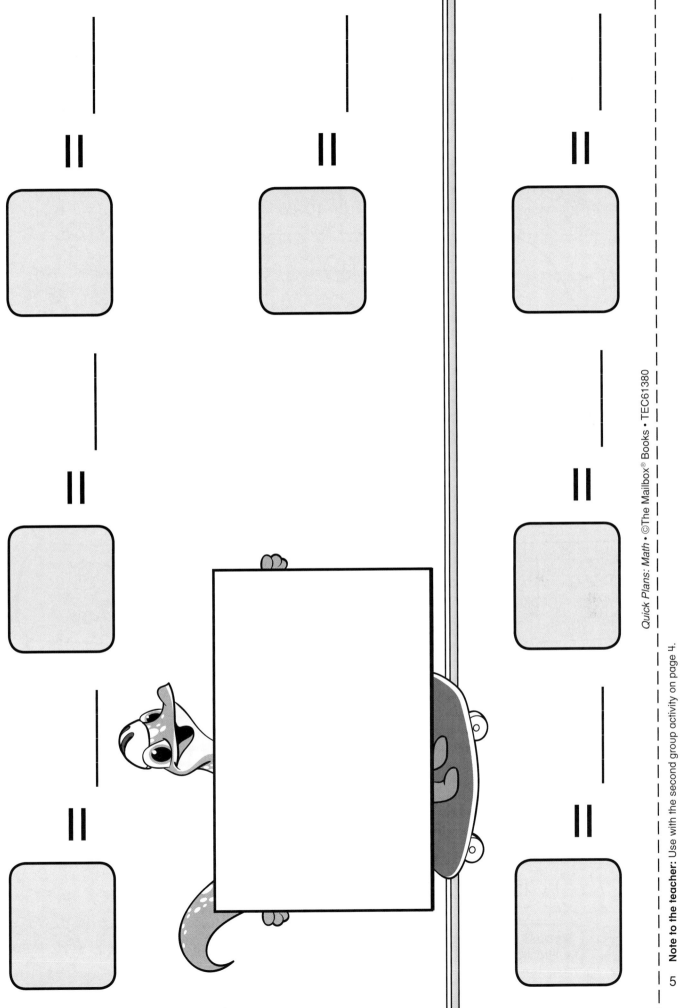

Quick Plans: Math • ©The Mailbox® Books • TEC61380

Note to the teacher: Use with the second group activity on page 4.

Buzzing Around

Add or subtract.
Color a bee with the matching answer.

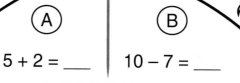

(A) 5 + 2 = ___   (B) 10 − 7 = ___

(C) 12 − 4 = ___   (D) 9 + 1 = ___   (E) 6 + 7 = ___

(F) 17 − 8 = ___   (G) 3 + 4 = ___   (H) 9 − 5 = ___   (I) 7 + 8 = ___

(J) 5 + 5 = ___   (K) 13 − 4 = ___   (L) 8 − 6 = ___   (M) 4 + 2 = ___

(N) 11 − 3 = ___   (O) 8 + 3 = ___   (P) 16 − 9 = ___   (Q) 4 + 9 = ___   (R) 14 − 8 = ___

(S) 1 + 3 = ___   (T) 8 − 2 = ___   (U) 12 − 5 = ___   (V) 9 + 4 = ___

(W) 15 − 7 = ___   (X) 2 + 3 = ___   (Y) 7 + 5 = ___   (Z) 12 − 7 = ___

Bonus: Find the uncolored bees. Use the numbers to write two addition and two subtraction problems. Solve each problem.

Quick Plans: Math • ©The Mailbox® Books • TEC61380 • Key p. 94

Addition and Subtraction Word Problems

Group Work

● Assign each child a different set of three related numbers. Have him use the numbers to write and illustrate a word problem. Then direct him to record the answer on the back of the paper. When everyone is finished, instruct each student to swap papers with a classmate, solve his partner's problem on scrap paper, and then check the answer. Repeat as desired.

● For several days, keep track of students' lunch choices, recess activities, and classroom scenarios. Then use that information to write a story problem on the board. Direct each student to write an equation for the problem, substituting a star for the missing number. Write students' different equations on the board and discuss how there can be more than one way to solve the problem. Then guide students to determine the answer.

On Tuesday, 6 students played kickball. On Wednesday, 10 students played kickball. How many more students played kickball on Wednesday?

$$6 + \star = 10$$
$$10 - 6 = \star$$

Centers

● Laminate two sheets of construction paper. Trim one sheet, program it as shown, and attach it to the inside of a box. Then trim the other sheet and attach it to the front of the box. Provide wipe-off markers, an eraser, and cards labeled with story problems. (Program the backs of the cards for self-checking.) A child chooses a card and writes the known information in the corresponding sections of the box. Next, he writes the answer in the remaining section of the box. The student flips the card over to check his work. Then he erases his numbers and chooses another card.

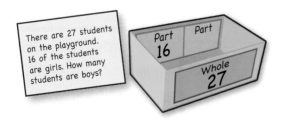

There are 27 students on the playground. 16 of the students are girls. How many students are boys?

Part 16 Part

Whole 27

● Label three bags as shown. Cut apart a copy of the cards from page 8 and place each set of cards in the corresponding bag. A student chooses one card from each bag and uses the information to write a word problem. Next, she writes a matching equation and solves it. She continues by choosing a new card from each bag.

First Number   Second Number   Directions

72   25   put together

Seatwork See page 9.

Word Problem Cards

Use with the second center activity on page 7.

First number	Second number	Directions
72	**28**	**add to**
TEC61380	TEC61380	TEC61380
65	**25**	**take from**
TEC61380	TEC61380	TEC61380
54	**6**	**put together**
TEC61380	TEC61380	TEC61380
58	**19**	**take apart**
TEC61380	TEC61380	TEC61380
49	**12**	**compare**
TEC61380	TEC61380	TEC61380

Pump It Up

Solve.
Show your work with pictures, words, or numbers.

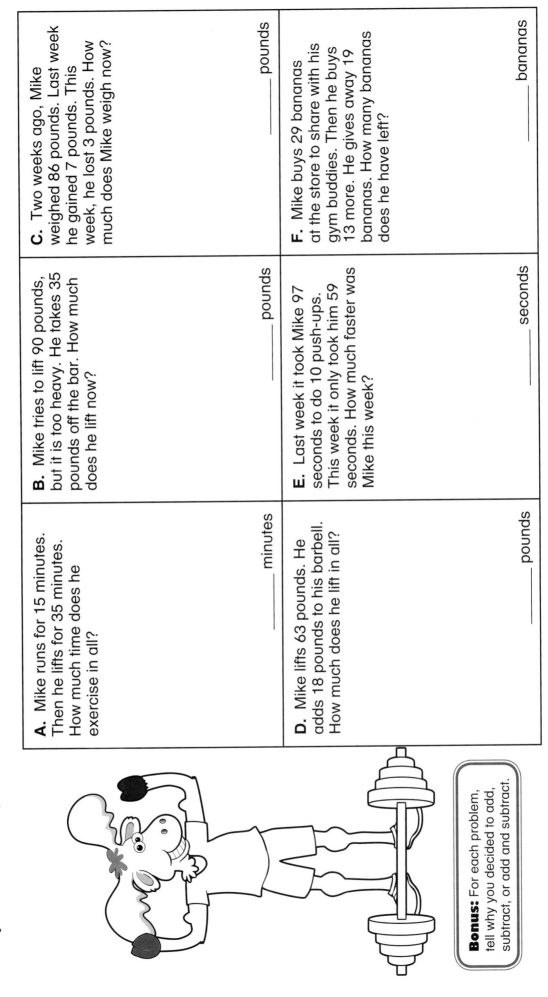

A. Mike runs for 15 minutes. Then he lifts for 35 minutes. How much time does he exercise in all?

_____ minutes

B. Mike tries to lift 90 pounds, but it is too heavy. He takes 35 pounds off the bar. How much does he lift now?

_____ pounds

C. Two weeks ago, Mike weighed 86 pounds. Last week he gained 7 pounds. This week, he lost 3 pounds. How much does Mike weigh now?

_____ pounds

D. Mike lifts 63 pounds. He adds 18 pounds to his barbell. How much does he lift in all?

_____ pounds

E. Last week it took Mike 97 seconds to do 10 push-ups. This week it only took him 59 seconds. How much faster was Mike this week?

_____ seconds

F. Mike buys 29 bananas at the store to share with his gym buddies. Then he buys 13 more. He gives away 19 bananas. How many bananas does he have left?

_____ bananas

Bonus: For each problem, tell why you decided to add, subtract, or add and subtract.

Multiplication

Group Work

● Draw a picture or array to illustrate a multiplication fact. Challenge each student to write and solve a corresponding addition sentence. When students are finished, invite a volunteer to write his sentence on the board and have the rest of the group confirm his work. Show the related multiplication fact. Draw a different picture on the board and continue in the same manner as time allows.

$$2 + 2 + 2 + 2 + 2 + 2 = 12$$
$$6 \times 2 = 12$$

● Provide each small group with a copy of the bug scene from page 11. Have each student identify the number of legs on each bug. Then have each group discuss strategies that could be used to find the total number of legs in the picture. Invite each group to share a different strategy. Then have them find the total number of legs. Repeat the activity using different bug characteristics, such as the number of eyes or stripes.

Centers

● Program a copy of the hand patterns from page 11 for each set of multiplication facts you would like students to practice. Laminate each paper and place them at a center with a multiplication table, a dry-erase marker, and an eraser. A child writes the answer to each fact on the corresponding finger or thumb. Then he checks his answers against the multiplication table before erasing his numbers.

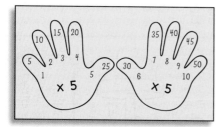

● *Partner Center:* Provide a laminated multiplication table, a deck of playing cards (face cards removed), and two different-colored wipe-off markers. Player 1 stacks the cards facedown and then takes the top two cards. Using aces as ones, she states the product of the numbers and then checks her answer on the multiplication table. If she is correct, she colors the corresponding chart space. If she is incorrect or none of the corresponding spaces are free, her turn ends. Alternate play continues until a student colors four spaces horizontally, vertically, or diagonally.

Seatwork See page 12.

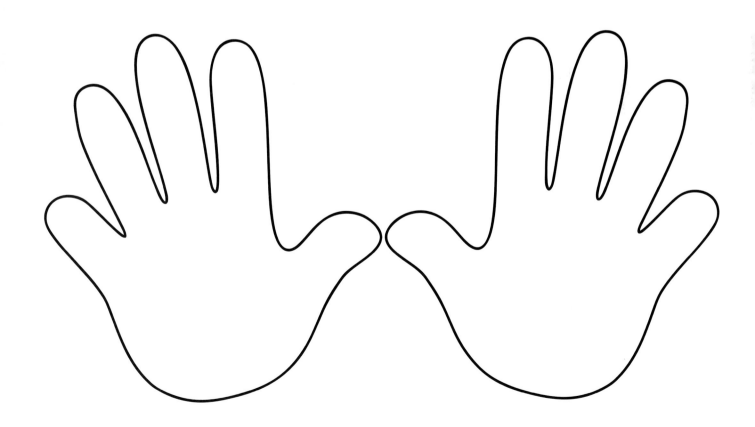

Note to the teacher: Use the scene at the top of the page with the second group activity on page 10. Use the hand picture with the first center activity on page 10.

A Tall Tower

Solve each problem using repeated addition.
Cross off the matching answer.

A. 2 x 6	$2 + 2 + 2 + 2 + 2 + 2 = 12$
B. 3 x 3	
C. 2 x 5	
D. 7 x 3	
E. 6 x 4	
F. 4 x 7	
G. 3 x 6	
H. 8 x 2	
I. 5 x 6	
J. 4 x 3	
K. 3 x 8	
L. 5 x 3	
M. 8 x 3	
N. 4 x 5	
O. 1 x 5	
P. 8 x 5	
Q. 2 x 9	
R. 5 x 7	
S. 9 x 6	
T. 7 x 7	

9	12
~~12~~	21
15	24
3	49
5	40
54	24
18	9
16	30
18	20
24	28
10	35

Bonus: Multiply the two remaining answers. Use repeated addition to find the product.

Division

Group Work

● Form small groups and give each group a supply of manipulatives, such as connecting cubes. Call out a dividend with numerous factors, such as 24. Challenge each group to use the corresponding number of cubes to determine all the possible division sentences for that dividend and list each division sentence. When a group finishes, a child holds up the list to be checked. Award a point to the team that finishes first and a point to the team with the most correct facts. Announce a different dividend to play another round. The group with the most points at the end of the game wins.

● Write a division problem on the board. Assign each student one of two strategies to solve it, such as subtraction or drawing a picture. Direct students to use their assigned strategies to solve the problem. When each child is finished, invite one student from each strategy group to reveal her results; then compare the results. Write a new problem on the board and have students solve this problem using the other strategy.

Centers

● Cut out a construction paper copy of the cookie patterns on page 14. Provide a cookie sheet and a supply of flash cards with dividends of 12 or less. A child chooses a flash card and divides the cookies into equal groups to match the problems. He draws a picture to match his cookie placement and then writes the corresponding division sentence.

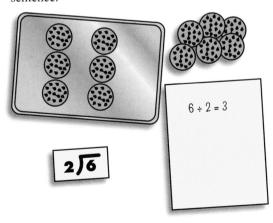

● Color a copy of the spinner on page 14 as indicated. Set out 12 red linking cubes, 18 blue linking cubes, 24 yellow linking cubes, and 30 green linking cubes. A child uses a paper clip and a pencil to spin the spinner. She takes the cubes that match the color spun and divides them into the number of groups shown on the spinner. Then she writes the corresponding division sentence on a sheet of paper. She spins again to repeat the activity.

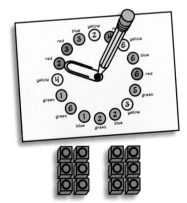

Seatwork See page 15.

Cookie Patterns

Use with the first center activity on page 13.

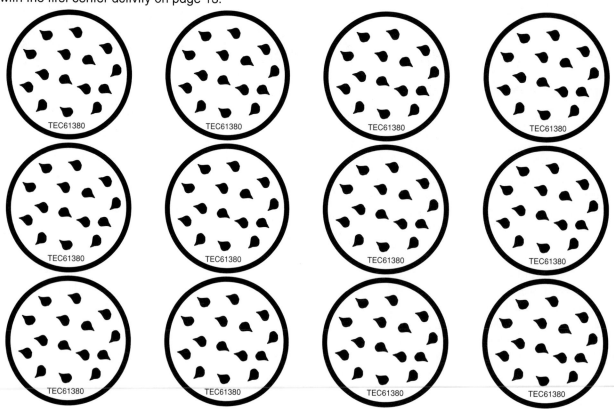

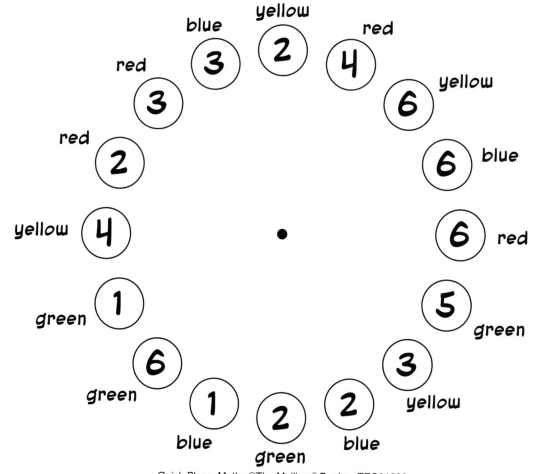

Quick Plans: Math • ©The Mailbox® Books • TEC61380

14   **Note to the teacher:** Use with the second center activity on page 13.

Name _____

Goody Gumballs

Draw an array to solve each problem.
Color a matching gumball.

For 10 ÷ 2, I can split ten into two equal groups.

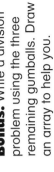

A. 10 ÷ 2 = 5 ⬭⬭⬭⬭⬭ ⬭⬭⬭⬭⬭	B. 8 ÷ 4 = □	C. 6 ÷ 6 = □
D. 12 ÷ 3 = □	E. 14 ÷ 7 = □	F. 20 ÷ 4 = □
G. 15 ÷ 5 = □	H. 8 ÷ 8 = □	I. 12 ÷ 2 = □
J. 16 ÷ 4 = □	K. 18 ÷ 3 = □	L. 9 ÷ 3 = □

Bonus: Write a division problem using the three remaining gumballs. Draw an array to help you.

Quick Plans: Math • ©The Mailbox® Books • TEC61380 • Key p. 94

15

Multiplication and Division Word Problems

Group Work

- Give each student a card from page 17, ensuring that each child's card matches another child's card. On your signal, direct students to find a classmate whose word problem or clue card matches his card. After a child finds his partner, instruct the pair to solve their problem on a sheet of paper. Then provide time for students to share their solutions.

- For each group, prepare a word problem that includes unnecessary information, listing each sentence on an individual paper strip. Form groups of four and assign each student a letter A–D. Student A puts the sentence strips in order. Student B removes the extra information strip. Student C writes an equation that solves the word problem. Student D draws a picture or an array that represents the solution.

Bobby mows 4 lawns on Saturday.

He charges $5 a lawn.

It takes Bobby 3 hours to cut all 4 lawns.

How much money does Bobby earn?

$$\$5 \times 4 = \$20$$

Centers

- Label each of three different-colored highlighters as shown; Also set out a class supply of individual multiplication and division word problems and manipulatives. A student selects a word problem and uses the highlighters to identify two different parts of the problem. Next, she models the problem with the manipulatives to find the solution. Then she writes an equation and draws the solution to the problem with the matching highlighter.

Farmer Ben has 24 quarts of milk. He milked 8 quarts from each cow. How many cows does Farmer Ben have?

Number of groups

Total

Number in each group

$$24 \div 8 = 3$$

- Provide magazines and catalogs. A student cuts out a picture of multiple items in a set—such as people, cars, or dogs—and he glues the picture to his paper. Next, the child writes a multiplication or division word problem about the picture, using one feature in the picture—such as the total number of arms, tires on cars, or ears on dogs—to develop the word problem. Then he writes an equation to solve the problem.

There are 6 children and 1 adult playing in the backyard. Each person kicked off their shoes and put the shoes in a pile. How many shoes are in the pile?

$7 \times 2 = 14$ shoes

Charlie

Seatwork See page 18.

Word Problem	Becky has 3 boxes in her desk. Each box has 6 pencils. How many pencils does Becky have? TEC61380	Clue	Number of groups: 3 Number in each group: 6 Total: ? TEC61380
Word Problem	Jordan has 20 stickers to give away. He gives an equal number of his stickers to 5 friends. How many stickers does each friend get? TEC61380	Clue	Number of groups: 5 Number in each group: ? Total: 20 TEC61380
Word Problem	Carly has 21 tennis balls. If she puts 3 tennis balls in each container, how many containers will she need? TEC61380	Clue	Number of groups: ? Number in each group: 3 Total: 21 TEC61380
Word Problem	Michael, Tim, and Lucas each score 8 points during the basketball game. How many points do they score altogether? TEC61380	Clue	Number of groups: 3 Number in each group: 8 Total: ? TEC61380
Word Problem	Alyssa has 24 books to put on her bookcase. She can only fit 6 books on each shelf. How many shelves will she use? TEC61380	Clue	Number of groups: ? Number in each group: 6 Total: 24 TEC61380
Word Problem	There are 28 students in Ms. Jones's class. She wants to put her students into 4 equal groups. How many students will be in each group? TEC61380	Clue	Number of groups: 4 Number in each group: ? Total: 28 TEC61380
Word Problem	Marco has 3 dogs and 12 dog treats. If he shares the treats equally, how many treats will Marco give each dog? TEC61380	Clue	Number of groups: 3 Number in each group: ? Total: 12 TEC61380
Word Problem	Nicholas colors 2 pictures for each of his cousins. He has 5 cousins in all. How many pictures does Nicholas color? TEC61380	Clue	Number of groups: 5 Number in each group: 2 Total: ? TEC61380
Word Problem	Claire bakes 15 cupcakes. She puts 5 cupcakes in each box. How many boxes of cupcakes does Claire have? TEC61380	Clue	Number of groups: ? Number in each group: 5 Total: 15 TEC61380

Name _____

Postman Peter

Solve each problem.
Show your work with pictures, words, or numbers.

A.
Two mailmen deliver mail. They each deliver 9 letters. How many letters do the mailmen deliver in all?

_____ letters

B.
Peter Pelican has 20 letters. He puts 5 letters in each mailbox. How many mailboxes get letters?

_____ mailboxes

C.
There are 8 houses on Water Street. Peter delivers 3 pieces of mail to each house. How many pieces of mail does Peter deliver?

_____ pieces of mail

D.
Peter stops at 4 apartments on Ocean Avenue. He puts 2 catalogs in each apartment's mailbox. How many catalogs does Peter deliver?

_____ catalogs

E.
Peter has 18 packages to deliver to 6 different people. Each person gets the same number of packages. How many packages does each person get?

_____ packages

F.
Peter has 15 stamps. He puts 3 stamps on each letter. How many letters get stamps?

_____ letters

Bonus: Write a multiplication word problem about 3 streets and 8 mailboxes. Then solve the problem.

Quick Plans: Math • ©The Mailbox® Books • TEC61380 • Key p. 94

Relating Multiplication and Division

Group Work

● Give each group a cut-out copy of the cards from page 20. Tell the class you will play music and, before the music stops, students must group their cards into number sets that can be used to make 12 different fact families. Begin playing a song such as "We Are Family" sung by Sister Sledge. Randomly stop the music. Have each student in the group write the fact families for three different sets of numbers.

● Have students cut two triangles from each of five paper squares. Direct each child to program her triangles with numbers and symbols from a multiplication fact family like the ones shown. Then assign partners and have the students quiz each other on their multiplication and division facts.

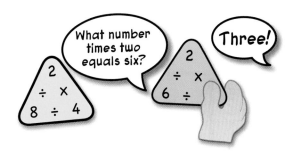

Centers

● Provide six multiplication flash cards and six related division flash cards. A student places each set of cards facedown. She turns over one card from each set and reads the fact on each card. If the cards belong to the same fact family, she writes and solves on her paper all four equations and then sets the cards aside. If the cards do not belong to the same fact family, she turns them back over and chooses another pair. The child continues until all the cards are matched and the fact families for each matching pair are written.

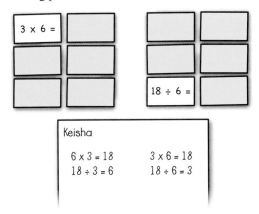

● Set out ads that show evenly divisible items for sale, such as three T-shirts for $12. A student divides a sheet of paper into four sections. He writes in the first section the name of an item and its advertised price. The child finds the unit price by writing a multiplication equation with an unknown whole number. After he solves for the unknown number, he writes the related division fact to check his work. The student repeats the process with three different ads.

2 bottles of orange
juice for $6

$2 \times ? = \$6$
$? = \$3$
$\$6 \div \$3 = 2$

Saul

Seatwork See page 21.

Number Cards

Use with the first group activity on page 19.

3	**7**	**21**	**2**	**8**	**16**
TEC61380	TEC61380	TEC61380	TEC61380	TEC61380	TEC61380
4	**6**	**24**	**5**	**9**	**45**
TEC61380	TEC61380	TEC61380	TEC61380	TEC61380	TEC61380
6	**3**	**18**	**7**	**4**	**28**
TEC61380	TEC61380	TEC61380	TEC61380	TEC61380	TEC61380
8	**5**	**40**	**9**	**6**	**54**
TEC61380	TEC61380	TEC61380	TEC61380	TEC61380	TEC61380
2	**10**	**20**	**3**	**11**	**33**
TEC61380	TEC61380	TEC61380	TEC61380	TEC61380	TEC61380
4	**12**	**48**	**5**	**1**	**5**
TEC61380	TEC61380	TEC61380	TEC61380	TEC61380	TEC61380

Flipping Flapjacks

Fill in the missing number.
Write a related division fact.

A. ( ) x 2 = 18 _____

B. 4 x ( ) = 20 _____

C. ( ) x 5 = 35 _____

D. 6 x ( ) = 24 _____

E. ( ) x 7 = 21 _____

F. 2 x ( ) = 6 _____

G. ( ) x 8 = 56 _____

H. 9 x ( ) = 36 _____

I. ( ) x 4 = 16 _____

J. 8 x ( ) = 48 _____

K. ( ) x 6 = 54 _____

L. 3 x ( ) = 15 _____

M. ( ) x 2 = 14 _____

N. 5 x ( ) = 25 _____

O. ( ) x 8 = 24 _____

P. 6 x ( ) = 36 _____

Q. 9 x ( ) = 72 _____

R. ( ) x 5 = 30 _____

S. 4 x ( ) = 28 _____

T. ( ) x 7 = 42 _____

Bonus: Write three multiplication and three related division problems. Use your age in each problem.

Commutative Property of Multiplication

Group Work

- Choose nine multiplication flash cards. Draw a 3 x 3 grid on the board, and for each card, label a grid space with the related multiplication problem. Then form two teams. Show Team 1 a flash card. The team members name the related problem and its product. If correct, Team 1 puts an X on the matching space. If incorrect, Team 2 tries to answer. If Team 2 is correct, the team puts an O on the matching space. If neither team is correct, set the card aside and revisit it later in the round. Alternate turns until one team gets tic-tac-toe or all the grid spaces are marked.

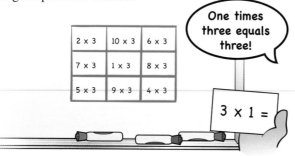

2 x 3	10 x 3	6 x 3
7 x 3	1 x 3	8 x 3
5 x 3	9 x 3	4 x 3

One times three equals three!

3 x 1 =

- Form groups of four. Give each group six small plastic cups and 30 dried beans. Direct the group to evenly distribute the beans among all six cups. Have students write the multiplication fact that represents the beans in the cups. Then have the students spill the beans from the cups and set aside one cup. Instruct the students to evenly redistribute the beans among the five cups and write the multiplication fact that represents the beans in the cups. Discuss how the product stayed the same but the order of the factors changed.

Centers

- Label a set of index cards A–F. On each card, glue a picture that represents equal groups. A student divides a sheet of paper into sixths and selects a picture card. She writes the letter of the card on her paper and writes the multiplication fact that represents the picture on the card. Then the student draws a picture to show a representation of the related fact.

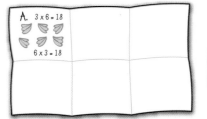

A. 3 x 6 = 18
6 x 3 = 18

A.

- Cut apart the puzzle cards on page 23 and place them in an envelope. A student matches the multiplication fact pieces together. Then, on a sheet of paper, he writes each problem and a matching illustration.

If...
4 x 7 = 28

Then...
7 x 4 = 28

So,
4 x 7 = 7 x 4

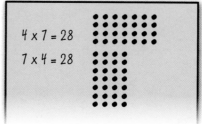

4 x 7 = 28
7 x 4 = 28

Seatwork See page 24.

Since	Then	So
4 x 7 = 28	7 x 4 = 28	4 x 7 = 7 x 4
TEC61380	TEC61380	TEC61380
Since	Then	So
5 x 9 = 45	9 x 5 = 45	5 x 9 = 9 x 5
TEC61380	TEC61380	TEC61380
Since	Then	So
3 x 6 = 18	6 x 3 = 18	3 x 6 = 6 x 3
TEC61380	TEC61380	TEC61380
Since	Then	So
7 x 9 = 63	9 x 7 = 63	7 x 9 = 9 x 7
TEC61380	TEC61380	TEC61380
Since	Then	So
4 x 8 = 32	8 x 4 = 32	4 x 8 = 8 x 4
TEC61380	TEC61380	TEC61380
Since	Then	So
5 x 7 = 35	7 x 5 = 35	5 x 7 = 7 x 5
TEC61380	TEC61380	TEC61380
Since	Then	So
6 x 9 = 54	9 x 6 = 54	6 x 9 = 9 x 6
TEC61380	TEC61380	TEC61380
Since	Then	So
4 x 9 = 36	9 x 4 = 36	4 x 9 = 9 x 4
TEC61380	TEC61380	TEC61380
Since	Then	So
3 x 8 = 24	8 x 3 = 24	3 x 8 = 8 x 3
TEC61380	TEC61380	TEC61380

Looking Back at You

Use the code to write and solve each problem.

For each pair, cross off the matching product.

Code

$\triangle$ = 6 $\bigcirc$ = 7 $\square$ = 8 $\heartsuit$ = 9

A. $\triangle$ x 1 = _____

    1 x $\triangle$ = _____

B. $\square$ x 3 = _____

    3 x $\square$ = _____

C. $\bigcirc$ x 5 = _____

    5 x $\bigcirc$ = _____

D. $\heartsuit$ x 2 = _____

    2 x $\heartsuit$ = _____

E. $\bigcirc$ x 4 = _____

    4 x $\bigcirc$ = _____

F. $\triangle$ x 3 = _____

    3 x $\triangle$ = _____

G. $\square$ x 5 = _____

    5 x $\square$ = _____

H. $\triangle$ x 4 = _____

    4 x $\triangle$ = _____

I. $\bigcirc$ x 3 = _____

    3 x $\bigcirc$ = _____

J. $\triangle$ x $\heartsuit$ = _____

    $\heartsuit$ x $\triangle$ = _____

K. $\bigcirc$ x $\square$ = _____

    $\square$ x $\bigcirc$ = _____

L. $\square$ x $\triangle$ = _____

    $\triangle$ x $\square$ = _____

M. $\bigcirc$ x $\triangle$ = _____

    $\triangle$ x $\bigcirc$ = _____

N. $\heartsuit$ x $\square$ = _____

    $\square$ x $\heartsuit$ = _____

O. $\bigcirc$ x $\heartsuit$ = _____

    $\heartsuit$ x $\bigcirc$ = _____

28   18   42   24

63   18

35   40   54   6   56

72   24   48   21

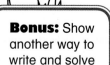

Bonus: Show another way to write and solve each problem.

    6 x 5

    8 x 6

    7 x 2

Associative Property of Multiplication

Group Work

- Make a supply of card stock fish templates (patterns on page 26). Guide each student to fold a 4" x 6" paper in half horizontally and place the template on top of the folded paper so that the fish's lips are along the fold. Direct the child to trace the template, cut it out, and unfold the paper. Next, have him write on each resulting fish a different way to solve the same three-factor multiplication equation. Display the fish with the title "Something's Fishy About These Facts."

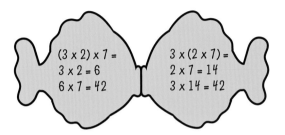

$(3 \times 2) \times 7 =$
$3 \times 2 = 6$
$6 \times 7 = 42$

$3 \times (2 \times 7) =$
$2 \times 7 = 14$
$3 \times 14 = 42$

- Form groups of three. Give each group a deck of playing cards with the face cards removed. One student deals 12 cards to each child. Then each child places his cards into four groups of three. She uses the numbers on her cards to write and solve multiplication equations using the associative property. When all students have written their problems, they return the cards to the deck. The dealer shuffles the cards, deals out 12 new cards, and students repeat the activity.

Centers

- Place a pair of dice and a supply of paper at a center. A student divides a sheet of paper into four columns and labels each one as shown. He rolls the dice three times and records in the first column each number he rolls. The child uses the numbers to write and solve in the second column a multiplication equation. Then, in the third column, he rearranges the same numbers and writes and solves a different equation. Finally, the student writes in the last column the product. He continues as time allows.

Numbers Rolled	Grouping 1	Grouping 2	Product
2, 3, 8	$(2 \times 3) \times 8$	$2 \times (3 \times 8)$	48
	$6 \times 8 = 48$	$2 \times 24 = 48$	

- Copy and cut out the cell phone pattern and cards from the bottom of page 26. A student shuffles the cards and stacks them facedown. She draws the top card and places it faceup at the top of her cell phone. Then she matches each letter of the word with the number on her cell phone keypad and uses the numbers to write and solve a multiplication equation. She checks her answer on a calculator and continues with the other cards.

LIP

LIP
$(5 \times 4) \times 7 =$
$5 \times 4 = 20$
$20 \times 7 = 140$

Seatwork See page 27.

Fish Patterns

Use with the first group activity on page 25.

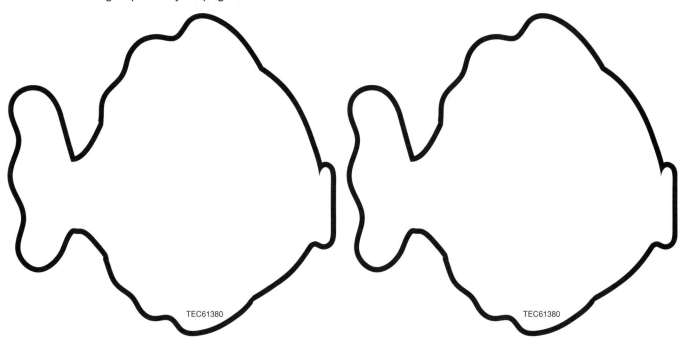

TEC61380   TEC61380

Cell Phone Pattern and Cards

Use with the second center activity on page 25.

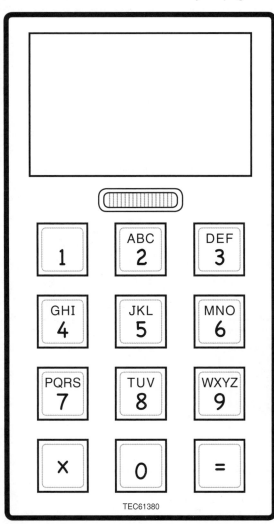

TEC61380

APE	CAR
TEC61380	TEC61380
DAD	EAR
TEC61380	TEC61380
HAT	LIP
TEC61380	TEC61380
MAD	YAK
TEC61380	TEC61380

Quick Plans: Math • ©The Mailbox® Books • TEC61380 • Key p. 94

A Puzzled Pirate

Write each missing number.
Then rewrite and solve each problem.

(3 x 2) x 4 = 3 x 2 = 6 6 x 4 = 24 ___3 x (2 x 4) = 24___ Ⓒ	8 x (2 x 5) = 2 x 5 = ☐ ☐ x 8 = ___ _____ Ⓖ	6 x (4 x 2) = 4 x 2 = ☐ ☐ x 6 = ___ _____ Ⓢ
(4 x 5) x 3 = 4 x 5 = ☐ ☐ x 3 = ___ _____ Ⓔ	(5 x 6) x 9 = 5 x 6 = ☐ ☐ x 9 = ___ _____ Ⓣ	(2 x 4) x 8 = 2 x 4 = ☐ ☐ x 8 = ___ _____ Ⓐ
(2 x 5) x 9 = 2 x 5 = ☐ ☐ x 9 = ___ _____ Ⓝ	(5 x 6) x 7 = 5 x 6 = ☐ ☐ x 7 = ___ _____ Ⓗ	6 x (3 x 2) = 3 x 2 = ☐ ☐ x 6 = ___ _____ Ⓘ
9 x (3 x 3) = 3 x 3 = ☐ ☐ x 9 = ___ _____ Ⓓ	7 x (5 x 8) = 5 x 8 = ☐ ☐ x 7 = ___ _____ Ⓦ	 No matter how you group the factors, the product stays the same. 

Why couldn't the pirate play a game of cards?

To solve the riddle, write the letters from above on the matching numbered line or lines.

Because ___ ___ ___ ___ ___ ___ ___ ___ ___ ___ ___ ___   O___
       210 60   280 64 48   48 36 270 270 36 90 80   90

              ___ ___ ___ ___ ___ ___K!
              270 210 60 81 60 24

Bonus: Show two different ways to find the product for 5 x 4 x 6.

Distributive Property of Multiplication

Group Work

● Have each group sort a copy of the cards on page 29 by matching symbols. After the cards are sorted, instruct the groups to remove the card in each set that does not belong. Direct one child in each group to record the symbol found on each matching pair of cards and write the multiplication fact that does not belong with each set.

● Form two groups. Give each group a bag of two different-colored Unifix cubes, a die, and a large sheet of paper. A student from each group rolls its die and announces the number to the other group. A recorder from each group writes the two numbers as a multiplication sentence and uses his group's input to separate one of the factors into two addends forming two new multiplication sentences. Next, each group uses its cubes to show an array for each product. The recorder draws the arrays and writes the equation represented by the drawing. Each group compares its findings with the other group.

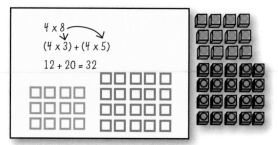

Centers

● Write on a paper strip the equation $(a \times b) + (a \times c)$ and set it out with a die and a set of dominoes. A student rolls to determine the value for a. She then selects a domino to find a value for b (the top dots of the domino) and a value for c (the bottom dots). The child writes an equation with the corresponding number values and a drawing of the domino. She solves each multiplication fact and adds the two products. Then, she writes the multiplication fact that is represented by the equation.

● Write the numbers 1 through 9 each on three different cards. Also program cards with distributive equation symbols (parenthesis, plus sign, multiplication sign, and equals sign). A student selects a flash card and uses the number and symbol cards to make a distributive property equation. Then he copies and solves the equation.

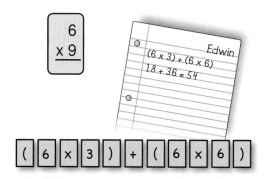

Seatwork See page 30.

☆	☆	☆
$(4 \times 2) + (4 \times 7)$	$(4 \times 3) + (4 \times 6)$	$(4 \times 1) + (4 \times 9)$
TEC61380	TEC61380	TEC61380

■	■	■
$(5 \times 6) + (5 \times 6)$	$(5 \times 3) + (5 \times 4)$	$(5 \times 5) + (5 \times 7)$
TEC61380	TEC61380	TEC61380

●	●	●
$(3 \times 1) + (3 \times 10)$	$(3 \times 4) + (3 \times 6)$	$(3 \times 5) + (3 \times 5)$
TEC61380	TEC61380	TEC61380

▲	▲	▲
$(2 \times 3) + (2 \times 4)$	$(2 \times 1) + (2 \times 7)$	$(2 \times 2) + (2 \times 5)$
TEC61380	TEC61380	TEC61380

♥	♥	♥
$(4 \times 3) + (4 \times 5)$	$(4 \times 4) + (4 \times 4)$	$(4 \times 2) + (4 \times 4)$
TEC61380	TEC61380	TEC61380

✿	✿	✿
$(5 \times 2) + (5 \times 5)$	$(5 \times 1) + (5 \times 7)$	$(5 \times 1) + (5 \times 6)$
TEC61380	TEC61380	TEC61380

◆	◆	◆
$(3 \times 3) + (3 \times 6)$	$(3 \times 4) + (3 \times 5)$	$(3 \times 3) + (3 \times 3)$
TEC61380	TEC61380	TEC61380

⬡	⬡	⬡
$(6 \times 4) + (6 \times 3)$	$(6 \times 7) + (6 \times 1)$	$(6 \times 5) + (6 \times 2)$
TEC61380	TEC61380	TEC61380

☾	☾	☾
$(8 \times 4) + (8 \times 5)$	$(8 \times 3) + (8 \times 6)$	$(8 \times 1) + (8 \times 9)$
TEC61380	TEC61380	TEC61380

Sunny Seeds

Write the product for each problem in the left column.

Find the problem in the right column that can help you check each product in the left column.

Write the matching letter on the seed.

A) $4 \times 9 =$

B) $2 \times 7 =$

C) $3 \times 9 =$

D) $5 \times 6 =$

E) $3 \times 5 =$

F) $4 \times 8 =$

G) $3 \times 7 =$

H) $6 \times 10 =$

I) $2 \times 8 =$

J) $5 \times 7 =$

K) $7 \times 4 =$

L) $6 \times 6 =$

M) $5 \times 9 =$

N) $4 \times 6 =$

O) $3 \times 6 =$

P) $6 \times 8 =$

$(2 \times 4) + (2 \times 3)$

$(5 \times 1) + (5 \times 5)$

$(3 \times 4) + (3 \times 2)$

$(2 \times 2) + (2 \times 6)$

$(4 \times 7) + (4 \times 1)$

$(6 \times 1) + (6 \times 5)$

$(6 \times 3) + (6 \times 7)$

$(7 \times 2) + (7 \times 2)$

$(4 \times 5) + (4 \times 4)$

$(3 \times 3) + (3 \times 4)$

$(5 \times 6) + (5 \times 3)$

$(4 \times 5) + (4 \times 1)$

$(6 \times 4) + (6 \times 4)$

$(3 \times 2) + (3 \times 3)$

$(5 \times 2) + (5 \times 5)$

$(3 \times 7) + (3 \times 2)$

To find the product, separate one factor into two addends. Multiply the two addends by the other factor. Then add the products.

To find the product of 2×9, I can think $2 \times (3 + 6)$. Then I solve: $(2 \times 3) + (2 \times 6) = 6 + 12 = 18$.

Bonus: Show two ways you can solve the problem 3×8 by using the equation $a \times (b + c)$.

 Quick Plans: Math • ©The Mailbox® Books • TEC61380 • Key p. 94

Two-Step Word Problems

Group Work

● Provide each group with a copy of a two-step word problem and several different-colored highlighters. Direct the group members to read the problem and determine the different steps involved. Then have the students highlight each step with a different color. Lead the children to work together to solve the problem. Then provide time for groups to compare and explain their thinking with the rest of the class.

● Write a list of clothing prices on the board; then give each group a shopping budget of $50. Direct each group to write and solve a two-step word problem that reflects a multiple purchase and the budget. Have each group share its word problems with the other groups and explain what two steps are needed to solve the problem.

Connor has $50. He wants to buy some new jeans for school. One pair of jeans costs $15. Connor buys three pairs. How much money does he have left?

jeans $15
shorts $8
T-shirt $7
sweatshirt $12
socks $3

Centers

● Cut apart a copy of the puzzle cards on page 32; put the word problem cards in one envelope and the answer cards in another envelope. A child solves each problem. Then he locates the answer card for each problem and fits the pieces together. He checks his work against the matching puzzle pieces. If his answer does not match the puzzle piece, he reworks the problem.

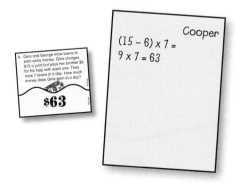

A. Gina and George mow lawns to earn extra money. Gina charges $15 a yard but pays her brother $6 for his help with each one. They mow 7 lawns in a day. How much money does Gina earn in a day?

$63

Cooper
(15 – 6) x 7 =
9 x 7 = 63

● Provide several copies of two-step word problems and 4" x 8" construction paper strips (three per child). A student stacks three paper strips, leaving one inch of each strip showing. She folds all three strips over until the top edge of the inside strip is one inch from the next strip; then she staples the booklet on the fold. The child labels each flap as shown. She selects a word problem, reads it, and draws a related picture on the first flap. Then the student completes the steps outlined on each tab to solve the problem.

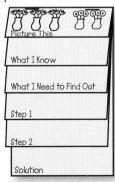

Picture This
What I Know
What I Need to Find Out
Step 1
Step 2
Solution

Seatwork See page 33.

Word Problem and Answer Puzzle Cards

Use with the first center activity on page 31.

A. Gina and George mow lawns to earn extra money. Gina charges $15 a yard but pays her brother $6 for his help with each one. They mow 7 lawns in a day. How much money does Gina earn in a day?

$63

B. Four friends bake the same number of cookies for the bake sale. They need 60 more cookies in order to sell 100 cookies. How many cookies did each friend already bake?

10

C. Lily makes 6 pitchers of lemonade to sell. Each pitcher holds enough lemonade to fill 9 cups. If Lily has 12 cups left, how many cups of lemonade did she sell?

42

D. Charlie makes 6 banana splits. Each banana split has 3 scoops of ice cream. If 9 scoops are chocolate, how many scoops are not chocolate?

9

E. A bag of potatoes has 20 potatoes. The Burger Palace uses 2 potatoes to make each order of french fries. If there are 8 bags of potatoes, how many orders of french fries can be made?

80

F. Zeke picks 78 apples. He puts the same number of apples in each basket. He fills 9 baskets and has 6 apples left over. How many apples are in each basket?

8

Name _____

Party Planning

Read.
Solve each problem. Show your work with pictures, numbers, or words.

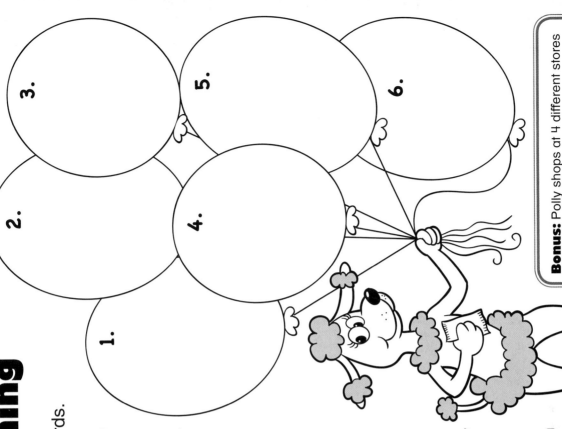

1. Polly invites 8 friends to her birthday party. She will give each friend 5 balloons. Polly buys packs of balloons with 4 balloons in each pack. How many packs of balloons does Polly buy? _____

2. Polly orders pizza for the party. Each pizza is cut into 6 slices. If Polly and her 8 friends can eat 2 slices each, how many pizzas should Polly order? _____

3. Polly's mother bakes 3 trays of cupcakes. Each tray holds 6 cupcakes. Polly has enough cupcakes to equally share among herself and her 8 guests. How many cupcakes will each guest get? _____

4. Polly has 2 bags of candy. Each bag has 20 pieces of candy. If Polly fills 8 goody bags with the same amount of candy, how many candy pieces does she put in each bag? _____

5. Polly needs juice boxes for the party. If she plans to have 4 juice boxes for each person and there are 9 people at the party, how many six-packs of juice should she buy? _____

6. Polly will play 3 games at her party. She and her guests will play 3 rounds of each game. Polly will give away 3 prizes at the end of each round. How many prizes does she need? _____

Place Value to 999

Group Work

● Number cards from 0 to 9. Invite three volunteers to hold a card and stand together. Discuss with students which child is standing in the ones, tens, and hundreds places. Then demonstrate how to write the number in expanded form by having the students in the tens and ones places hold their arms up so they resemble zeros. Write the resulting number on the board and direct the child that was in the hundreds place to sit on the floor. Repeat this process with the remaining numbers, writing addition symbols where applicable. Direct the students to stand together to make the number again and compare it to the expanded form.

● Laminate a copy of an expanded form strip from page 35 for each child and direct him to fold it as shown. Write a number on the board and have each child use a dry-erase marker to copy the number onto his folded strip. Guide students to open their strips and fill in the blank spaces to write the number in expanded form. Direct each child to refold the strip and say the number; then have him unfold the strip and read aloud the matching expanded form.

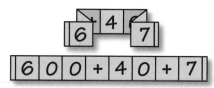

Centers

● Set out a spinner similar to the one shown along with cards labeled with a variety of three-digit numbers and a paper clip. A child chooses a card and spins the spinner. Starting with the number on her card, she skip-counts based on her spin, writing each number on a sheet of paper. She continues the pattern until she has written five numbers or until the number is close to zero.

● Set out copies of the recording sheet on page 35 and a variety of furniture, electronics, and appliance sales flyers. A student cuts two items from the sales flyers and glues one on each half of her paper. Then she draws on the recording sheet dollar bills to match each price. She compares the prices of the two items and draws the appropriate symbol between them.

Seatwork See page 36.

			+			+	
			+			+	
			+			+	

TEC61380

100s	10s	1s	100s	10s	1s

Quick Plans: Math • ©The Mailbox® Books • TEC61380

Note to the teacher: Use with the second center activity on page 34.

Picking Posies

Compare the number on each petal to the flower's boldfaced number.
Color each petal by the code.

Color Code
petal > bold number—pink
petal < bold number—orange
petal = bold number—yellow

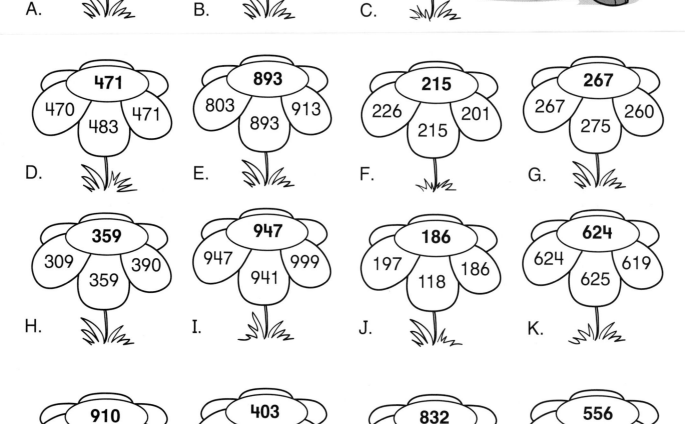

A. **195** — 184, 195, 199

B. **308** — 380, 301, 308

C. **724** — 724, 729, 720

D. **471** — 470, 471, 483

E. **893** — 803, 913, 893

F. **215** — 226, 201, 215

G. **267** — 267, 260, 275

H. **359** — 309, 390, 359

I. **947** — 947, 999, 941

J. **186** — 197, 186, 118

K. **624** — 624, 619, 625

L. **910** — 901, 910, 925

M. **403** — 473, 395, 403

N. **832** — 832, 854, 817

O. **556** — 563, 528, 556

Bonus: Circle each flower in which all the numbers are greater than 500.

Quick Plans: Math • ©The Mailbox® Books • TEC61380 • Key p. 94

Rounding Numbers

Group Work

Form two teams and have each team stand in a line. Announce a rounding rule and direct the first student from each team to stand at the board. Randomly open a book and announce the page number. The first student to correctly write the rounded number on the board earns a point for her team. Repeat the process with the next pair of students. Play continues until one team earns a predetermined number of points.

Cut out a copy of the baseball player pattern from page 38. Label a sticky note with a desired number and attach it to the player; then draw on the board two bases with a line between them. Announce a rounding rule and have students help you label the bases and the line according to the rule. Tape the baseball player along the line; then guide students to determine which base the player is closer to. Then have a volunteer move the baseball player to the appropriate base.

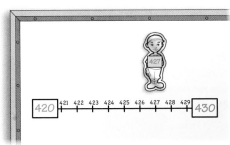

Centers

Draw on a large sheet of paper a lasso shape. Next label cow cards (page 38) with a different number; then write on the back whether the number gets rounded up or down to the nearest ten. A child chooses a card and rounds the number to the nearest ten. If he rounds the number up, he places the card inside the lasso to "round up the cow." If he rounds the number down, he places the card outside the lasso. He continues with each card and then turns them over to check his work.

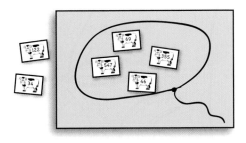

Program a sheet of construction paper as shown and slip it into a plastic sheet protector. Also provide a wipe-off marker, a pair of dice, and a laminated mountain climber cutout (pattern on page 38). A child rolls the dice and uses the wipe-off marker to write a resulting two-digit number on the mountain climber. Then he writes the numbers for rounding to the nearest ten in each box. He places the climber in its approximate location. If the mountain climber has not made it to the top of the mountain or further, the child rounds the number down. If the mountain climber makes it to the top of the mountain or over, the child rounds the number up. He writes the original number and the rounded number on a sheet of paper.

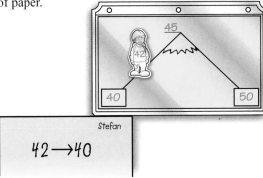

Seatwork See page 39.

Baseball Player Pattern

Use with the second group activity on page 37.

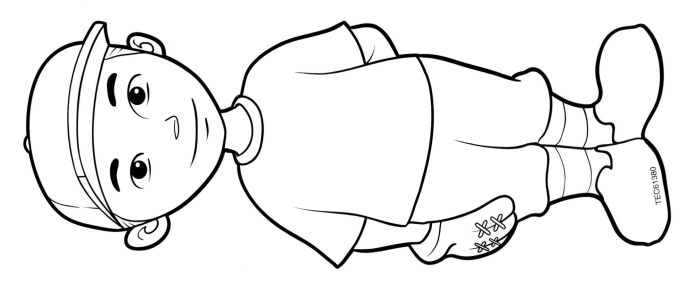

Cow Cards

Use with the first center activity on page 37.

Mountain Climber Pattern

Use with the second center activity on page 37.

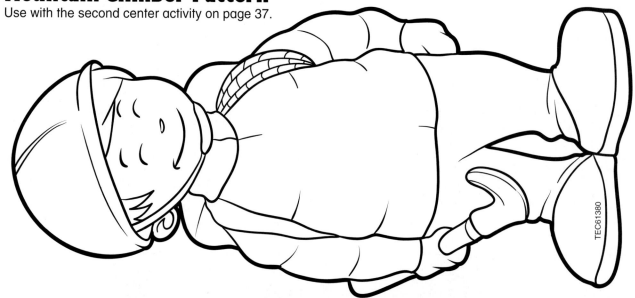

Name _____

What a Race!

Follow the directions.

Remember: If the digit to the right of the place you're rounding to is 5 or more, round up!

Round to the nearest 10.

23	51	89	18	61	93	36	25	45	57

Round to the nearest 10.

965	192	784	243	435	138	857	622	361	713

Round to the nearest 100.

645	916	452	691	142	779	324	287	828	373

Bonus: Who won the race? To find out, circle each number you rounded up. The racer with the most circled numbers is the winner.

Fluently Add and Subtract Within 100

Group Work

- Cut apart the numbers from a copy of a hundred chart and place them in a jar. Each day, draw two cards and write the numbers on the board, either in ascending or descending order. If the numbers are in ascending order, instruct students to add the numbers. If the numbers are in descending order, have students subtract the numbers.

- Form groups and give each group two dominoes. Each group arranges its dominoes side by side and then each group member copies and solves the addition problem. The groups repeat the steps to make a different addition problem and two subtraction problems.

$$\begin{array}{r} 53 \\ + 12 \\ \hline 65 \end{array}$$

Centers

- **Partner Game:** Label ten Unifix cubes with a different number from 0 to 9 and put the cubes in a bucket. Students take turns selecting four cubes. Each child uses her cubes to make two two-digit numbers that will produce a sum or difference that is close to 100 without going over. She writes her equation on her paper; then she compares her answer to her partner's answer. The student whose answer is closer to 100 earns a point. If a player's answer is over 100, her partner earns another point. The students return the cubes to the bucket and play another round. The child with more points at the end of play wins.

- Copy, laminate, and cut out the patterns from page 41. Also set out a dry-erase marker and an eraser. A student selects three scoops that he thinks will have a sum less than 100 and stacks them on a cone. He adds all three numbers together and writes the sum on the cone. Then he sets aside the completed cone and repeats the activity until six cones are made.

Mandi
$$\begin{array}{r} 87 \\ - 46 \\ \hline 41 \end{array}$$

Tori
$$\begin{array}{r} 39 \\ + 21 \\ \hline 60 \end{array}$$

Seatwork See page 42.

Ice Cream Scoop and Cone Patterns

Use with the second center activity on page 40.

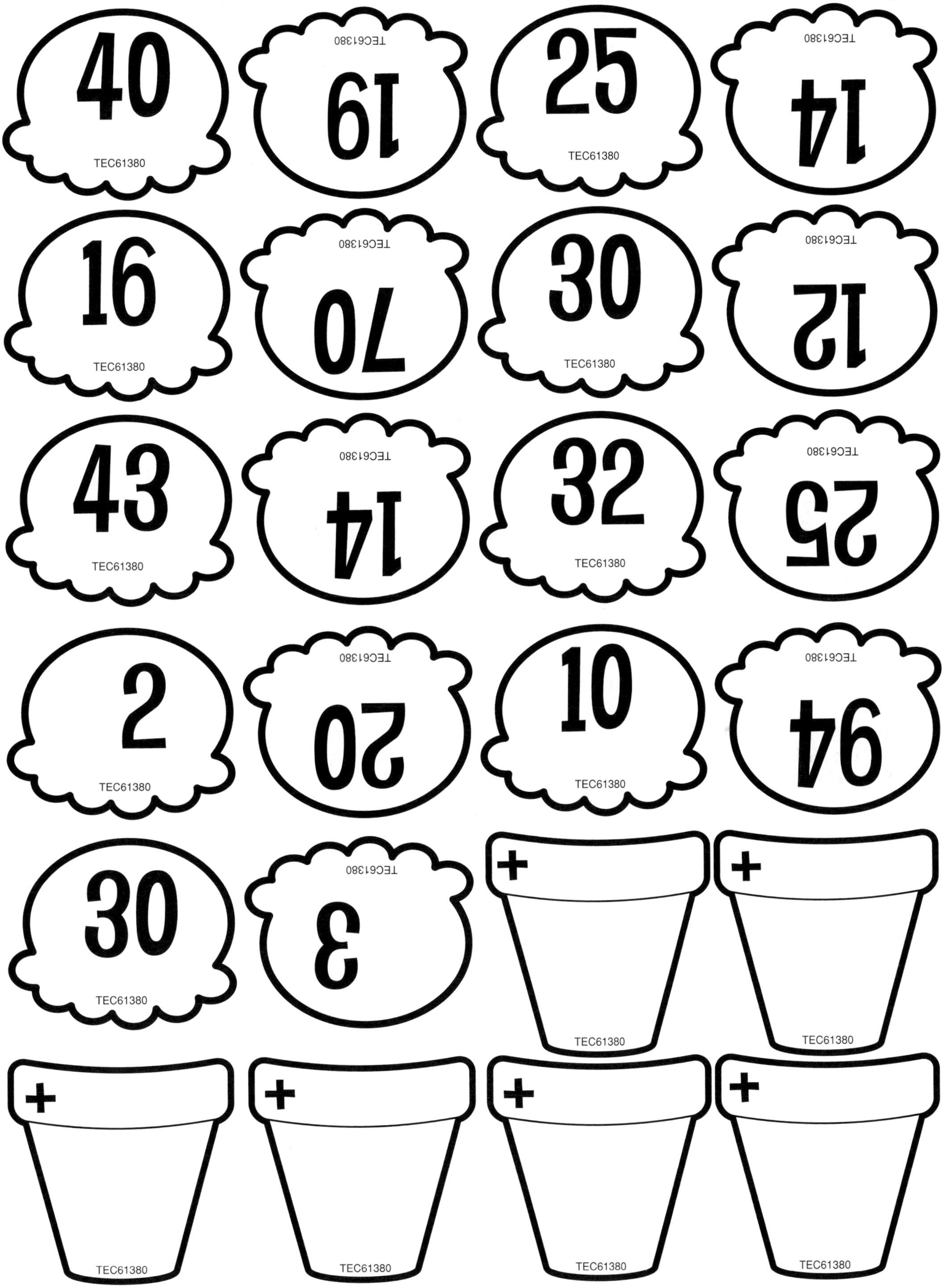
40
TEC61380
19
TEC61380
25
TEC61380
14
TEC61380
16
TEC61380
70
TEC61380
30
TEC61380
12
TEC61380
43
TEC61380
14
TEC61380
32
TEC61380
25
TEC61380
2
TEC61380
20
TEC61380
10
TEC61380
94
TEC61380
30
TEC61380
3
TEC61380
+
TEC61380
+
TEC61380
+
TEC61380
+
TEC61380
+
TEC61380
+
TEC61380

Name_____

Climbing for Coconuts

Add or subtract.
Write each answer in the matching boxes, placing one
    digit in each box.
Hint: One digit of each answer is also in the next answer.

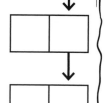

A.
```
    14
    32
  + 26
```

B.
```
    81
  - 19
```

C.
```
    48
    10
  + 34
```

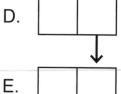

D.
```
    65
  + 26
```

E.
```
    70
  - 29
```

F.
```
    13
     8
  + 27
```

G.
```
    82
  - 44
```

H.
```
    54
  - 15
```

I.
```
    11
    49
  + 19
```

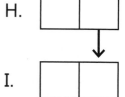

J.
```
    93
  - 18
```

K.
```
    28
    30
  +  7
```

L.
```
    86
  - 19
```

A.
B.
C.
D.
E.
F.
G.
H.
I.
J.
K.
L.

Bonus: What strategies did you use to add more than two addends?

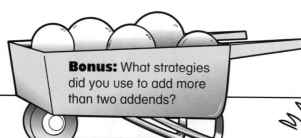
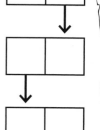

Quick Plans: Math • ©The Mailbox® Books • TEC61380 • Key p. 95

Fluently Add and Subtract Within 1,000

Group Work

● Give each student a copy of the gameboard on page 44. Direct youngsters to write above each letter of "PLAY TO WIN" a number between 100 and 200. Write on the board three different addition problems, such as $P + W$ =, $A + O$ =, and $Y + N$ =. Instruct each student to write on the chart the numbers from the top of his paper that match the letters in the three addition problems. Have him solve each problem and then add the three sums to get a total score for the round. Then play Round 2.

● Display the numbers shown. Each student writes on a sheet of paper two addends from the "Add" column and calculates the sum. Then, on your signal, each child passes her paper to the student on her right. That child selects a number from the "Subtract" column and subtracts it from the sum. Continue the activity, having students alternate between the two columns and choosing only unused numbers. At the end of the activity, students return the papers to their original owners, who check that the final answer equals 748.

Add	Subtract
346	278
297	345
508	169
189	206
472	417
351	

Centers

● Copy five flower patterns from page 44 and label each petal with an addend. Find the sum of the numbers on each flower; then write each sum on a separate milk cap. A student selects a flower, finds the sum of the numbers on the petals, and places the matching cap in the flower's center. She continues until all the milk caps are matched with their flowers.

● Copy each number shown onto a separate index card. Also provide a novelty coin. A child stacks the cards facedown; then turns over the top two cards. He flips the coin and, if the coin lands on heads, uses the numbers to solve an addition problem on his paper. If the coin lands on tails, he subtracts the numbers. After solving, the child sets the cards aside and turns over the next two cards.

37	99	162	186	234
273	315	404	498	500

Seatwork See page 45.

Flower Pattern

Use with the first center activity on page 43.

TEC61380

Fluently add within 1,000

Game On!

P L A Y T O W I N

Round 1

___ + ___ = ___

___ + ___ = ___

___ + ___ = ___

Total:

Round 2

___ + ___ = ___

___ + ___ = ___

___ + ___ = ___

Total:

Quick Plans: Math • ©The Mailbox® Books • TEC61380

Note to the teacher: Use with the first group activity on page 43.

Just One Scoop!

Add or subtract.
Use your answers to complete each puzzle.

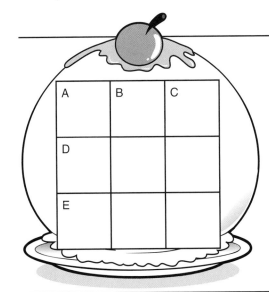

Across

A.	987	D.	214	E.	865
	− 159		+ 295		− 672

Down

A.	314	B.	536	C.	659
	+ 537		− 327		+ 234

Across

F.	364	I.	496	J.	785
	+ 218		+ 108		− 288

Down

F.	925	G.	172	H.	721
	− 361		+ 637		− 474

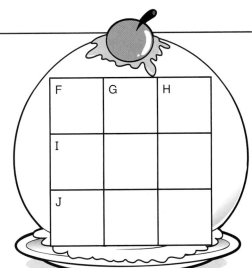

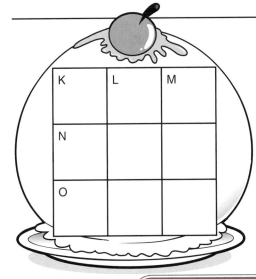

Across

K.	839	N.	607	O.	728
	− 456		− 465		− 135

Down

K.	152	L.	473	M.	598
	+ 163		+ 376		− 275

Bonus: Look back at problem N. Explain how to subtract from a zero.

Multiply by Multiples of 10

Group Work

- Provide each student with 12 plastic or paper dimes. Have each student use her dimes to show a set equal to 30. Then have her show an additional set of 30 with her dimes. Invite students to discuss how they might use the sets to find the total amount of dimes, leading them to understand that two groups of 30 equal six tens, or 60. Repeat the activity with different multiples of ten and ask students to volunteer examples.

- Make a gameboard like the one shown. Also cut apart a copy of the game cards on page 47; then gather a die and two game markers. Form two teams. In turn, each team draws a card, reads it aloud, and solves the problem. If the team's answer is correct, a team member rolls the die and moves the team's game marker. If the answer is incorrect, the team's turn ends. The game ends when one team reaches the finish line.

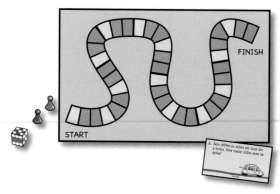

Centers

- **Partner Game:** Program 12 index cards each with a different multiplication problem that has a multiple of ten as one of the factors. Provide ink daubers and a calculator. The student pair stacks the cards facedown and Player 1 draws the top card. He copies and solves the problem on his paper, using an ink dauber instead of a handwritten zero. Player 2 uses the calculator to check the answer. If Player 1 is correct, he keeps the card; if Player 1 is incorrect, Player 2 takes the card. Then Player 2 takes her turn. The game continues until there are no more cards to be played. The player with more cards wins the game.

- Provide a supply of small stickers. A student traces his left and right hands on a sheet of paper and then puts a sticker on each fingertip. Next, the child writes in order from left to right the multiples of ten as shown. The student uses the mat to practice multiplying by ten.

One, two, three, four...ten times four equals 40.

Seatwork See page 48.

A. Sam drives 50 miles per hour for 4 hours. How many miles does he drive?

TEC61380

B. Gus drives to work 40 miles one way. How many miles does he drive to and from work?

TEC61380

C. Rachel rides her bike 20 miles a day for 1 week. How many miles does she ride in a week?

TEC61380

D. Joy and 3 friends take turns driving. They switch drivers every 90 miles. If each person gets only 1 turn to drive, how many miles is the trip?

TEC61380

E. It takes Carlos 3 hours to get from City A to City B. If Carlos drives 60 miles per hour, how many miles is it between the 2 cities?

TEC61380

F. Mica spends $30 on a tank of gas each time he fills his car. Mica fills his car's gas tank 4 times on his trip. How much does Mica spend on gas?

TEC61380

G. If Jenna takes 1 hour to bike 80 miles, how many miles can she travel in 6 hours?

TEC61380

H. The Parkers live 70 miles from the beach. If they travel back and forth from their house to the beach on Saturday and Sunday, how many miles will they have traveled?

TEC61380

I. Cal puts 50 miles on his scooter in June. If he travels the same number of miles every month, how many miles will he travel on his scooter in 7 months?

TEC61380

J. Nate listens to the radio while driving his car. His favorite radio station plays 20 songs every hour. How many songs will Nate hear on his 5-hour trip?

TEC61380

Take a Bite

Multiply.

20 x 8	50 x 6	70 x 2	80 x 5
L	O	B	H
40 x 9	70 x 7	40 x 3	90 x 6
T	R	H	A
50 x 4	60 x 7	30 x 3	20 x 9
K	A	E	T
80 x 4	50 x 9	60 x 4	90 x 7
F	B	Y	O
30 x 5	80 x 8	20 x 4	70 x 3
V	O	H	T

How is a tree like a big dog?

To solve the riddle, write the letter above the matching numbered line or lines.

‾‾‾ ‾‾‾ ‾‾‾ ‾‾‾
360 80 90 240

‾‾‾ ‾‾‾ ‾‾‾ ‾‾‾   ‾‾‾ ‾‾‾ ‾‾‾ ‾‾‾
450 300 210 400 120 540 150 90

‾‾‾   ‾‾‾ ‾‾‾ ‾‾‾   ‾‾‾ ‾‾‾
540   160 640 180 630 320

‾‾‾ ‾‾‾ ‾‾‾ ‾‾‾!
140 420 490 200

Bonus: Circle the two-digit products from above. Multiply each product by your grade. Show your work.

Quick Plans: Math • ©The Mailbox® Books • TEC61380 • Key p. 95

Representing Fractions

Group Work

● Post a list of sight words that have two, three, four, six, or eight letters. Review the words with students and count the number of letters in each word, writing each word's total next to it. Pose questions such as "Which word is ¾ *l*'s?" or "Which word is ½ *f*'s?" Have students tell you the word or words and explain their reasoning.

● Gather five different-colored sentence strips and cut each one into equal pieces to represent different fractions: halves, thirds, fourths, sixths, and eighths. Pass out the pieces. Then tape a whole sentence strip to the board and label its ends "0" and "1" (number line). Name a fraction and direct students to tape the matching pieces below the number line. Then label each fraction on the number line. Continue with other fractions.

0       $\frac{1}{3}$ $\frac{2}{3}$ 1

Centers

● Make student copies of the top of page 50. A student divides a sheet of blank paper into six equal sections. Next, he colors matching fraction cards the same color and then cuts them apart. The child assembles the cards to make fraction bars and glues each fraction bar to a different section of his paper. Then he labels each section with the matching term. Finally, the student writes in the bottom section observations he makes about the fractions.

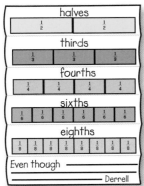

● Place the following crayons in a plastic bag: five green, four red, three blue, two yellow, and one purple. Also provide a copy of the fraction tasks on page 50 and two dice. A child rolls the dice, writes the number on a sheet of paper, and reads the corresponding fraction task. She refers to the crayons to determine the answer and draws a picture to show her results. The child also writes the fractional answer. She rolls the dice and completes three more tasks.

Seatwork See page 51.

Fraction Bar Cards

Use with the first center activity on page 49.

| $\dfrac{1}{2}$ | | $\dfrac{1}{4}$ | $\dfrac{1}{4}$ |

| $\dfrac{1}{3}$ | $\dfrac{1}{6}$ | $\dfrac{1}{6}$ | $\dfrac{1}{3}$ |

| $\dfrac{1}{4}$ | $\dfrac{1}{8}$ | $\dfrac{1}{4}$ | $\dfrac{1}{8}$ | $\dfrac{1}{8}$ | $\dfrac{1}{8}$ |

| $\dfrac{1}{6}$ | $\dfrac{1}{3}$ | $\dfrac{1}{6}$ | $\dfrac{1}{6}$ | $\dfrac{1}{6}$ |

| $\dfrac{1}{8}$ | $\dfrac{1}{8}$ | $\dfrac{1}{8}$ | $\dfrac{1}{8}$ | $\dfrac{1}{2}$ |

TEC61380

Roll, Review, and Write
Representing Fractions

2. Group the red and yellow crayons. What fraction is yellow?

3. Group the blue and purple crayons. What fraction is blue?

4. Group the yellow, purple, and blue crayons. What fraction is blue?

5. Group the green and purple crayons. What fraction is green?

6. Group the purple and green crayons. What fraction is purple?

7. Group the red and yellow crayons. What fraction is red?

8. Group the blue crayons. What fraction is blue?

9. Group the yellow crayons. What fraction is red?

10. Group the green and blue crayons. What fraction is green?

11. Group the red, blue, and purple crayons. What fraction is purple?

12. Group the purple and yellow crayons. What fraction is yellow?

Note to the teacher: Use with the second center activity on page 49.

50

Cakes and Candles

Circle the fraction for the shaded part of each cake.

A. $\frac{3}{4}$ or $\frac{1}{4}$

B. $\frac{1}{8}$ or $\frac{4}{8}$

C. $\frac{1}{8}$ or $\frac{7}{8}$

D. $\frac{6}{8}$ or $\frac{3}{8}$

E. $\frac{5}{6}$ or $\frac{4}{6}$

F. $\frac{1}{3}$ or $\frac{2}{3}$

G. $\frac{4}{6}$ or $\frac{2}{6}$

H. $\frac{3}{8}$ or $\frac{5}{8}$

I. $\frac{1}{3}$ or $\frac{2}{3}$

J. $\frac{3}{6}$ or $\frac{5}{6}$

K. $\frac{2}{4}$ or $\frac{1}{4}$

L. $\frac{1}{8}$ or $\frac{7}{8}$

Write the circled fractions from above on the candles
to complete the number lines.
(Hint: Two fractions will not be used.)

M.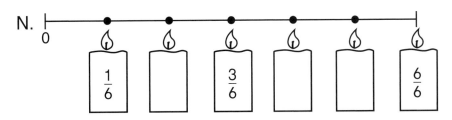

N.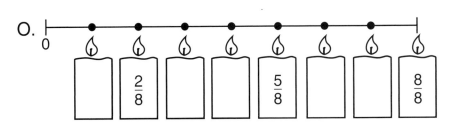

I sure hope it's banana cake!

Bonus: Draw two square cakes. Show $\frac{1}{3}$ shaded on one. Show $\frac{2}{3}$ shaded on the other.

O.

Comparing Fractions

Group Work

● Have each child fold and label a sheet of paper as shown. Write a fraction on the board and have the student copy it in the first column. Announce another fraction and have the child create a number sentence by saying the fraction in the first column and repeating the fraction named. Have him write the named fraction in the corresponding column. Continue with other fractions; then reveal the correct answers.

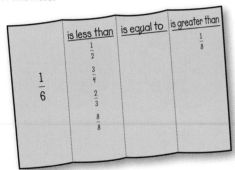

● Prepare a spinner by dividing a paper plate into five sections and writing one denominator (2, 3, 4, 6, and 8) in each section. Form small groups and tell students each group will make a poster showing equal values. One child from each group uses a paper clip and a pencil to spin the spinner two times. Her group members use the numbers spun as the denominators for their posters. Then each group creates a poster that shows two equivalent fractions. Provide time for groups to share their work.

Centers

● Copy the bird pattern on page 53 and cut it out. Turn the bird over and use a marker to add an eye and beak outline. Also copy the worm cards from the same page and cut them apart. A child takes two worms. He compares the fractions and places the bird between the worms so that its mouth is open to the larger fraction. The student copies the expression on his paper and then sets the worms aside. He continues until all the worms have been used.

● *Partner Game:* Cut apart two copies of the worm cards on page 53. Player 1 deals all the cards facedown. To start, Player 2 counts down from three. After he says "one," both players turn over their top cards. If the two fractions are equivalent, the first player to put a hand on the cards takes the cards; if the fractions are not equal, the students set the cards aside. Then Player 1 starts a new round by counting down from three. Students continue until all the cards are played. The player with more sets of equivalent fractions wins.

Seatwork See page 54.

Bird Pattern

Use with the first center activity on page 52.

TEC61380

Worm Cards

Use with the center activities on page 52.

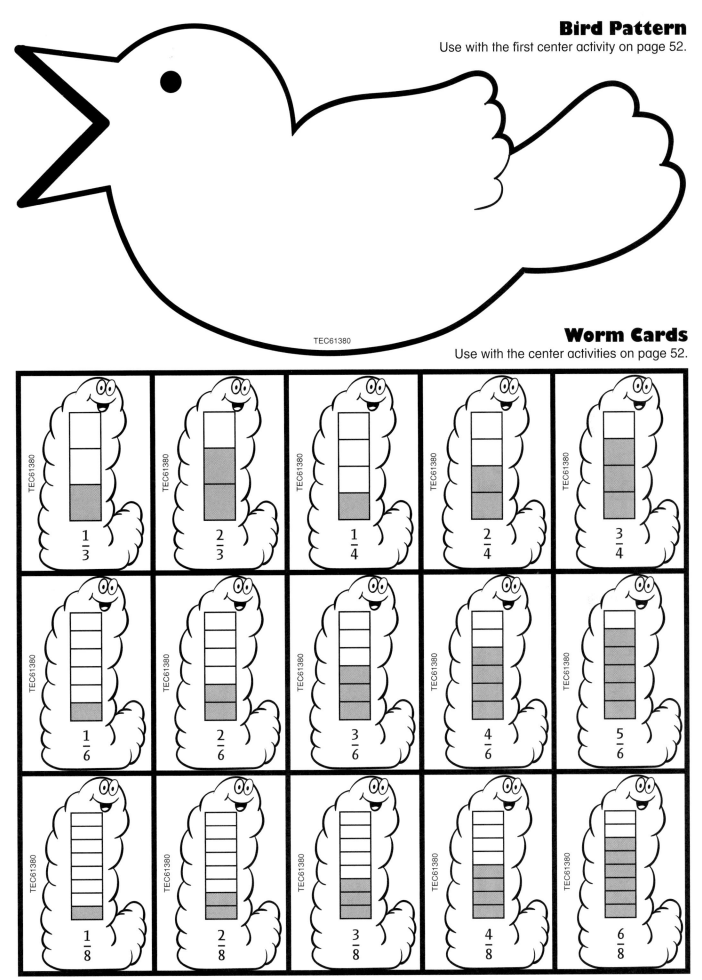

Name _____

The "Two-Can" Paint Company

Color the paint cans to show each fraction.
Write < or > to compare the cans in each set.

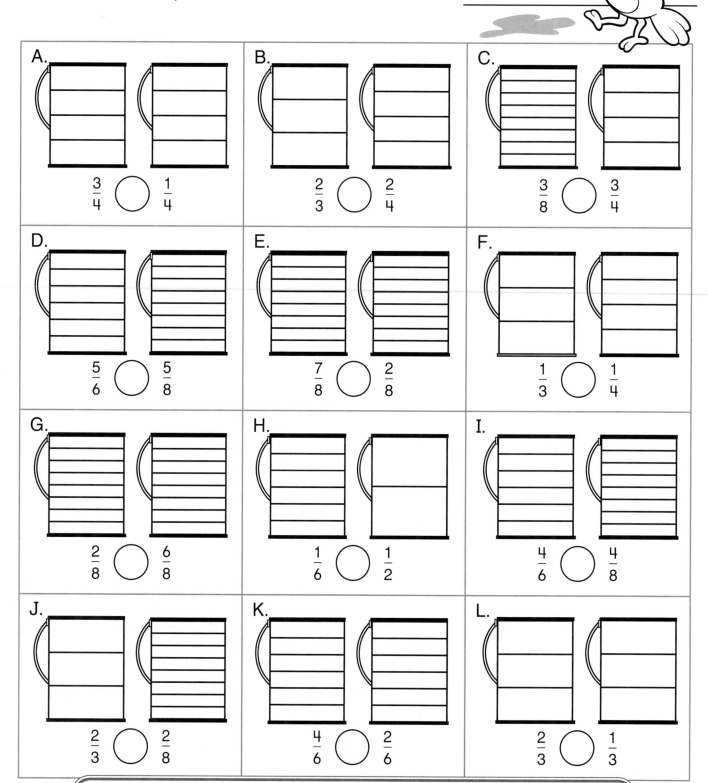

Bonus: Tara Toucan has 3 cans of paint. One is $\frac{1}{4}$ full. Another is $\frac{1}{2}$ full, and the third is $\frac{1}{8}$ full. Draw the cans. Circle the can with the least paint.

Length

Group Work

● Use masking tape to make a starting line and a finish line. Form teams and place a game marker, such as a plastic cup, for each team on the starting line. Then give each team a collection of objects that vary in length (glue sticks, paper clips, erasers, shoelaces, and blocks). Name an object and a unit of measure. Direct the teams to record an estimate of the object's length on a sheet of paper and then use a ruler to measure the object's actual length. The team whose estimate is closest to the actual measurement moves its game marker the same distance as the object's length. Repeat with different items until one team reaches the finish line.

● Gather objects with different lengths. Form teams and display the point system shown. Hold up an object and call out a unit of measure. Direct one student from each team to estimate the length of the object and record her team's estimate on a sheet of paper. Then have another student measure the actual length of the object and announce the measurement. Check and score each team's estimate according to the point system. Repeat the activity with the remaining objects. The team with the lowest score wins!

exact measurement = 0 points
1-unit difference = 1 point
2-unit difference = 2 points
3-unit difference = 3 points
4-unit or more difference = 4 points

Centers

● Make a copy of the spinner and cube pattern on page 56. Assemble the cube. Also set out a paper clip, a ruler, a meter stick, and a supply of paper. A student rolls the cube to determine the length of an object she will need to find. Then she spins the spinner to name the unit in which the object will be measured. The child records the object's name and estimate. Then she measures the object with the appropriate measuring tool and records the actual measurement. She repeats the steps five or more times.

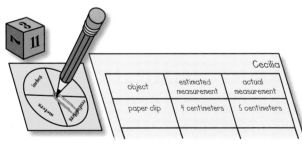

object	estimated measurement	actual measurement
paper clip	4 centimeters	5 centimeters

Cecilia

● A student divides a sheet of paper into fourths and writes the sentence starter shown across the center. He labels each section with a different unit of measure and, inside each section, draws and labels objects that relate to the unit of measure.

Seatwork See page 57.

Spinner and Cube Pattern

Use with the first center activity on page 55.

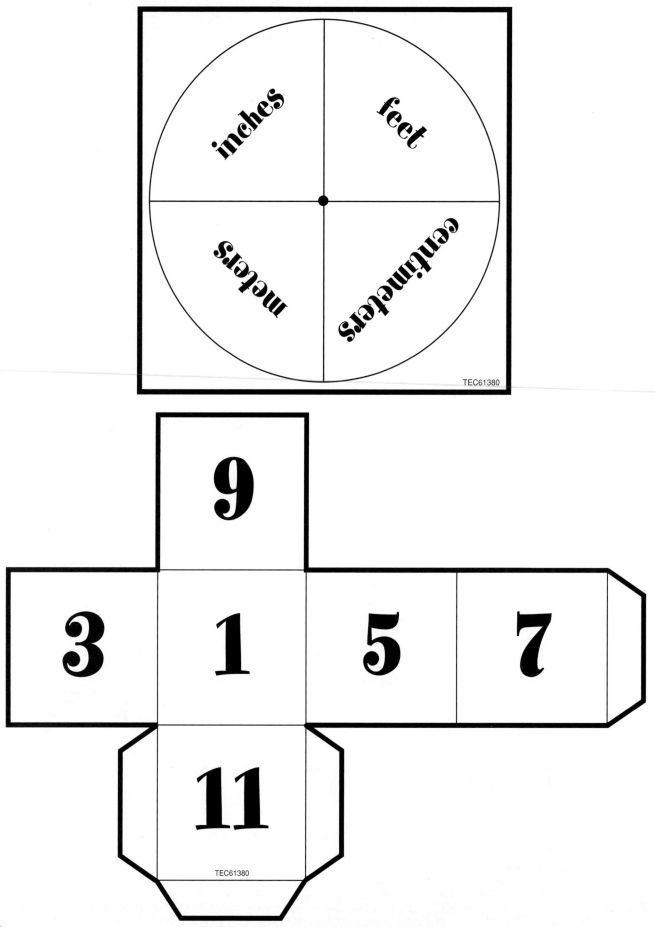

TEC61380

TEC61380

Hiking in the Woods

Estimate the height of each tree to the nearest $\frac{1}{2}$ inch.
Then use a ruler to measure the actual height of each tree.

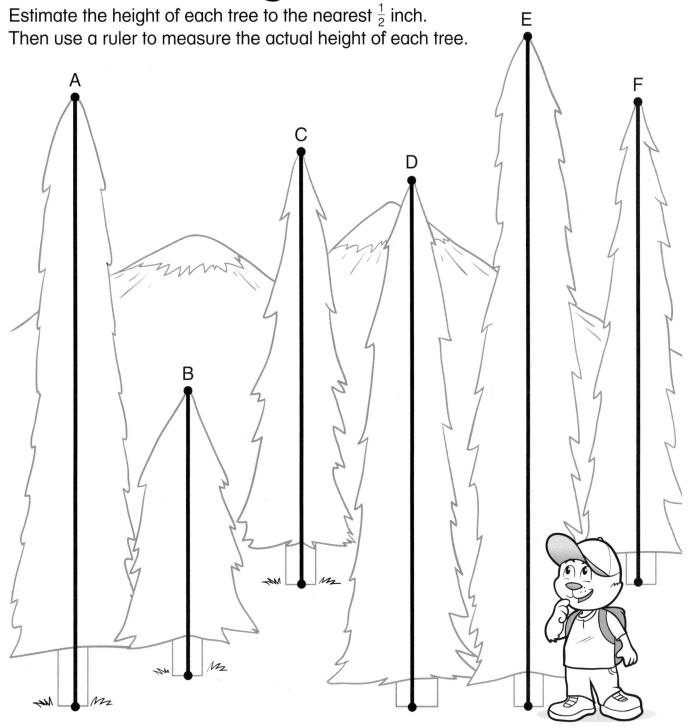

tree	estimate	actual
A	inches	inches
B	inches	inches
C	inches	inches

tree	estimate	actual
D	inches	inches
E	inches	inches
F	inches	inches

Bonus: What is your estimate of the distance in inches between tree trunks A and E? What is the actual distance?

Length Word Problems

Group Work

- Cut a variety of chenille stems (caterpillars) into different lengths. Give each student a caterpillar and a ruler. Form groups of three or four. Instruct each child to measure the length of his caterpillar and share the measurement with his group. Have each student use two of the caterpillar lengths to create a word problem that combines or compares the caterpillars. Then direct the groups to exchange and solve the word problems. Guide students to return the solved word problems to the original group to have the answers checked.

- Use masking tape to create a starting line on the floor. Form two teams and have them line up behind the starting line. One student from each team stands with his toes touching the starting line while holding a piece of masking tape. On your cue, each student jumps as far as he can and places the tape at the back of his heels. Then both children use a yardstick to measure to the nearest inch the distances they jumped. Both students return to their seats and use their measurements to write and solve an original word problem that compares the two distances. Invite student pairs to share their word problems with the other students.

  > Juan jumped 18 inches. Matt jumped 14 inches How many more inches did Juan jump than Matt?
  >
  > 18 – 14 = 4 inches

Centers

- A student draws a picture of herself with an exaggerated length of hair, writes a word problem about getting a haircut, and shows the equation that solves the problem. The child writes the answer in the bottom right corner of the paper and tapes colored paper over the answer to create a flap. Then she hole-punches her paper and places it inside a binder to make a class book of word problems. When each child has written a word problem, have students revisit the center to solve the problems.

- Cut various lengths of paper strips (each less than 100 centimeters) and label each strip with a letter. Cut apart student copies of the number lines on page 59; then copy the word problem shown onto an index card. Also provide a meter stick. A student selects a strip and measures it with the meter stick. On his paper, he writes the letter of the strip; then he copies the word problem and inserts his name and the length of the strip. Next, the child glues a number line below the word problem, draws the strip's length across the top of the number line, and uses the number line to model his answer. He writes an equation that reflects his understanding of the solution.

Anna's hair is 17 inches long. She gets a haircut. The hairstylist cuts off 6 inches of Anna's hair. How long is Anna's hair now?

17 – 6 = ?
Answer:

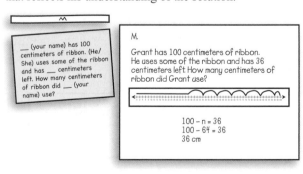

___ (your name) has 100 centimeters of ribbon. (He/She) uses some of the ribbon and has ___ centimeters left. How many centimeters of ribbon did ___ (your name) use?

M.

Grant has 100 centimeters of ribbon. He uses some of the ribbon and has 36 centimeters left. How many centimeters of ribbon did Grant use?

100 – n = 36
100 – 64 = 36
36 cm

Seatwork See page 60.

Five vertical number lines, each marked from 0 to 100 in increments of 2:

0 2 4 6 8 10 12 14 16 18 20 22 24 26 28 30 32 34 36 38 40 42 44 46 48 50 52 54 56 58 60 62 64 66 68 70 72 74 76 78 80 82 84 86 88 90 92 94 96 98 100

TEC61380

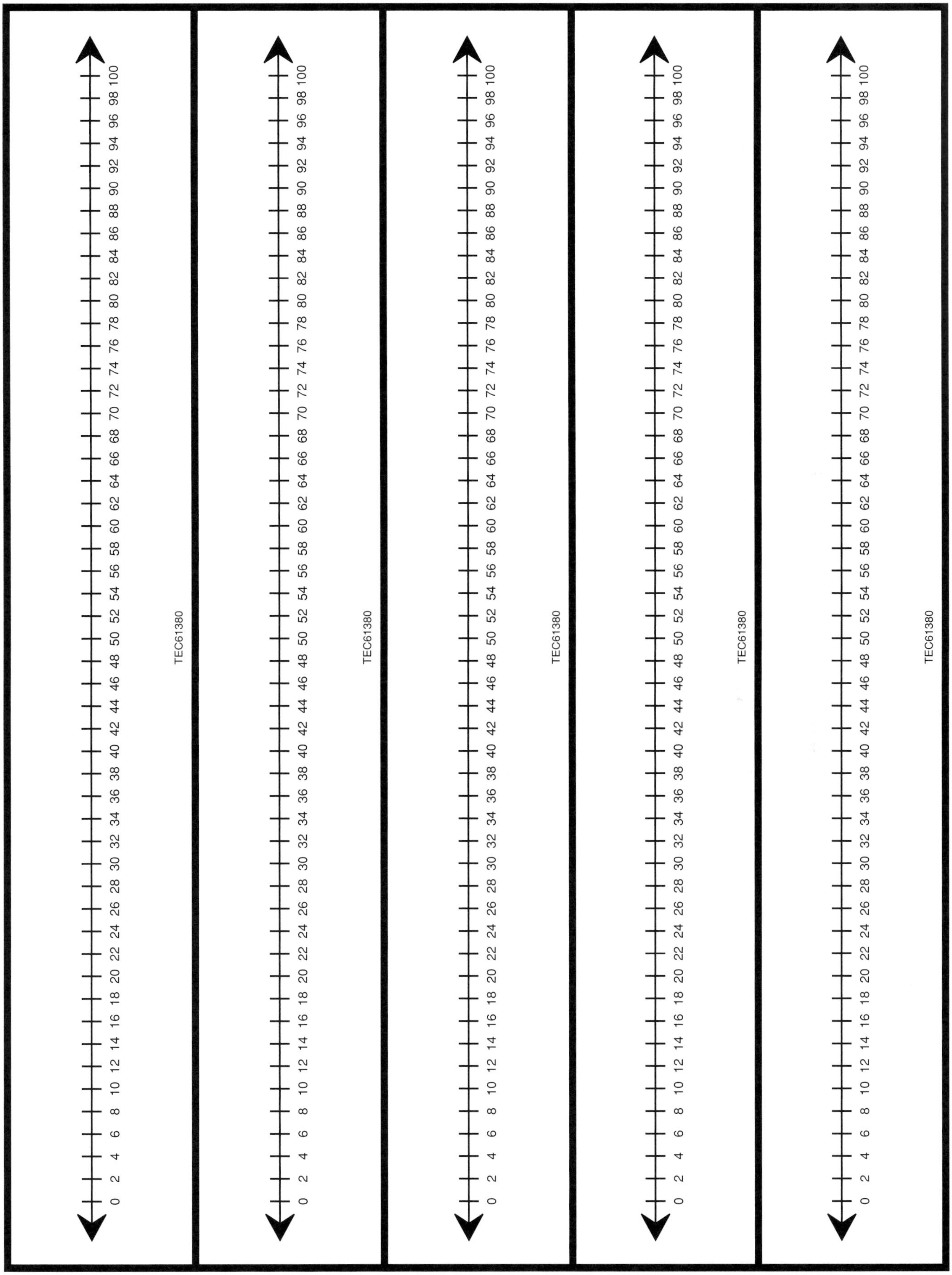

Word problems: addition and subtraction within 100 to solve for length

Inching Along

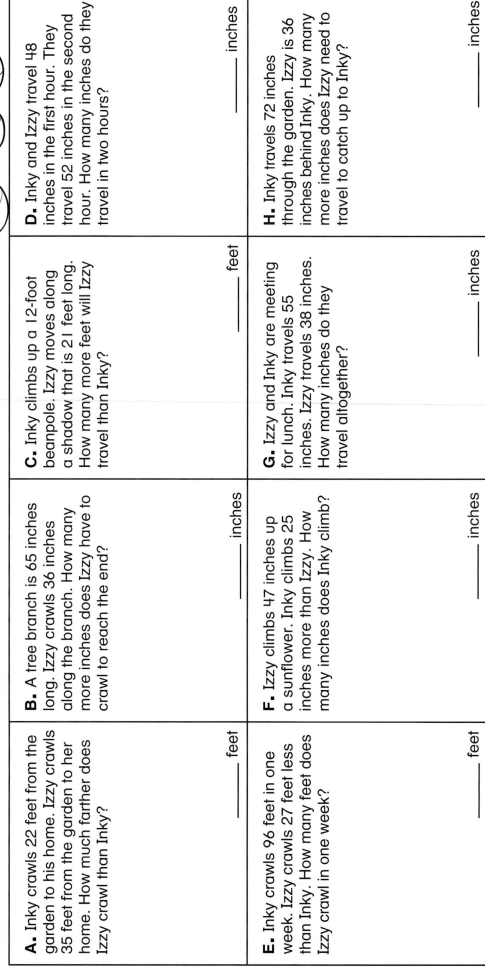

Write an equation.
Then solve the problem.

A. Inky crawls 22 feet from the garden to his home. Izzy crawls 35 feet from the garden to her home. How much farther does Izzy crawl than Inky?

_____ feet

B. A tree branch is 65 inches long. Izzy crawls 36 inches along the branch. How many more inches does Izzy have to crawl to reach the end?

_____ inches

C. Inky climbs up a 12-foot beanpole. Izzy moves along a shadow that is 21 feet long. How many more feet will Izzy travel than Inky?

_____ feet

D. Inky and Izzy travel 48 inches in the first hour. They travel 52 inches in the second hour. How many inches do they travel in two hours?

_____ inches

E. Inky crawls 96 feet in one week. Izzy crawls 27 feet less than Inky. How many feet does Izzy crawl in one week?

_____ feet

F. Izzy climbs 47 inches up a sunflower. Inky climbs 25 inches more than Izzy. How many inches does Inky climb?

_____ inches

G. Izzy and Inky are meeting for lunch. Inky travels 55 inches. Izzy travels 38 inches. How many inches do they travel altogether?

_____ inches

H. Inky travels 72 inches through the garden. Izzy is 36 inches behind Inky. How many more inches does Izzy need to travel to catch up to Inky?

_____ inches

Bonus: Use the equation 34 + ___ = 82 inches to write a word problem about Inky and Izzy.

Volume and Mass

Group Work

● Have each group cut out a copy of the cards from the bottom of page 62. Instruct the group members to match each picture to a reasonable unit of measure on the mat. After each group has placed all its cards, have groups take turns sharing which pictures they matched with which measurement. Allow time for discussion if two or more groups disagree with a match.

● Gather five clear containers of different sizes (each less than 1000 mL) and shapes and label the containers A through E. Fill each container with water and add a drop of different-colored food coloring to each one. Hold up container A; then have each child write on his paper an estimate in milliliters for the amount of liquid it holds. Pour the contents of container A into a 1,000 milliliter graduated cylinder. Ask a volunteer to read aloud the resulting measurement and have the students record it on their papers. Continue until all five containers have been estimated and measured.

container	estimate	actual measurement
A	300 milliliters	250 milliliters

Centers

● Gather six clean margarine tubs with lids and six objects with different weights. Put one object in each tub. Cover the tubs with their lids and tape them securely. Number the bottom of the tubs from lightest (1) to heaviest (6). A student chooses two tubs and determines which is the heavier tub. She continues comparing tubs, lining them in order from lightest to heaviest. When she has them arranged, she checks the order by carefully flipping the tubs over.

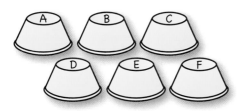

golf ball	rock
magnet	seashell
paper clip	wooden block

● Set out a balance scale and several small objects (paper clip, seashell, marble, table tennis ball, button, feather, cotton ball). A student takes a paper clip and another object; then he writes on a sheet of paper a prediction of how the objects' masses compare. He places each object on a different side of the balance scale; then he records his findings. The student repeats the steps until all objects are compared to the paper clip.

Seatwork See page 63.

Fill It Up!

75 liters	**180** milliliters	**5** liters	**355** milliliters	**4** liters
480 milliliters	**2** liters	**15** liters	**37** liters	**300** milliliters
200 liters	**360** milliliters	**1** liter	**240** milliliters	**749** liters

TEC61380

juice box TEC61380	water bottle TEC61380	soda can TEC61380	coffee cup TEC61380	soup bowl TEC61380
jar TEC61380	fish bowl TEC61380	milk jug TEC61380	vase TEC61380	large pot TEC61380
sink TEC61380	fish tank TEC61380	garbage can TEC61380	bathtub TEC61380	swimming pool TEC61380

A Bubbly Burglar

Circle the letter of the best estimate for each object.

object	estimated measurement	
1. bowl of soup	A. 300 milliliters	N. 3 liters
2. apple	K. 180 grams	P. 18 kilograms
3. small fishbowl full of water	H. 5 milliliters	D. 5 liters
4. textbook	C. 100 grams	O. 1 kilogram
5. can of soda	E. 355 milliliters	D. 3 liters
6. watermelon	L. 40 grams	N. 4 kilograms
7. bucket of water	T. 4 milliliters	M. 4 liters
8. television	E. 13 grams	H. 13 kilograms
9. full kid's swimming pool	W. 750 milliliters	L. 750 liters
10. laptop computer	N. 300 grams	C. 3 kilograms
11. bathtub full of water	A. 15 milliliters	Y. 150 liters
12. cell phone	G. 140 grams	T. 4 kilograms
13. bathroom sink full of water	M. 80 milliliters	W. 8 liters
14. golf ball	T. 45 grams	O. 4 kilograms

1,000 mililiters = 1 liter
1,000 grams = 1 kilogram

Bonus: List 3 containers that hold less than 1 liter. List 3 objects that weigh more than 1 kilogram.

Why did the burglar take a bath before robbing the bank?
To solve the riddle, write the circled letters on the matching numbered line or lines below.

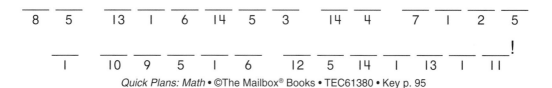

___ ___ ___ ___ ___ ___ ___ ___ ___ ___ ___ ___ ___ ___
 8   5   13 1   6 14   5   3   14   4   7   1   2   5

___ ___ ___ ___ ___ ___ ___ ___ ___ ___ ___ ___ ___!
 1   10   9   5   1   6   12   5 14   1 13   1 11

Time

Group Work

- Set 12 chairs in a circle and label each one with a different interval of five (0 through 55). Select 12 students to stand inside the circle. Begin playing a fun song, such as "Rock Around the Clock" sung by Bill Haley and His Comets, and direct students to move clockwise inside the circle (clock). Stop the music and instruct students to take a seat in the closest chair. Say a time to the nearest five minutes and have students outside the clock determine who is seated at the matching five-minute interval. Have that student leave the circle and select another student to take his place.

- Cut apart a copy of the time cards from page 65. Select one student to be the "fox" and the remaining students the "hens." Instruct the hens to stand in a line across the front of the room while holding a manipulative clock. Have the fox stand with the cards at the back of the room. To begin, the hens ask, "What time is it, Mr. Fox?" The fox draws a card and reads the time aloud. The hens set the time on their clocks, and the fox checks each hen's clock against the analog clock on the card. Hens with the correct answer take one step forward toward the fox. Play continues until a hen reaches the fox.

Centers

- Program a class set of paper strips with different times. Place the strips, a circle template, and a supply of drawing paper at a center. A student selects a paper strip, copies the time onto her paper, and adds "AM" to the time. She traces a circle and draws a matching analog clock. Above the time, she draws and labels a picture of a morning event that takes place at that time. Then the child turns her paper over, copies the time and "PM," and then draws an afternoon or evening event for that time.

- *Partner Game*: Cut apart a card stock copy of the time cards on page 65. Label two paper plates as shown. Also set out a handheld analog clock manipulative and two paper clips. Each player slides a paper clip onto the 12 on a paper plate. Player 1 shuffles the cards and stacks the deck facedown. Player 2 draws a card and reads the time to Player 1. Player 1 sets the hands on the analog clock to show the time. Player 2 checks the hands' placement against the card. If Player 1 is correct, he moves his paper clip to the next hour (1). If Player 1 is incorrect, his turn ends. Then Player 1 draws a card and reads the time to Player 2. The first player to return his paper clip to the 12 wins.

Seatwork See page 66.

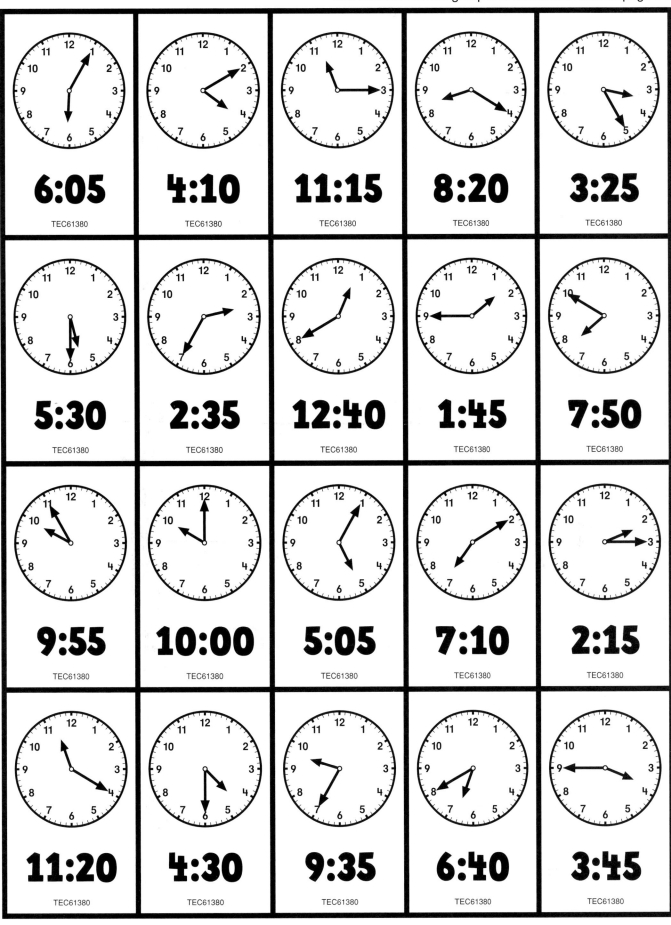

6:05 — TEC61380

4:10 — TEC61380

11:15 — TEC61380

8:20 — TEC61380

3:25 — TEC61380

5:30 — TEC61380

2:35 — TEC61380

12:40 — TEC61380

1:45 — TEC61380

7:50 — TEC61380

9:55 — TEC61380

10:00 — TEC61380

5:05 — TEC61380

7:10 — TEC61380

2:15 — TEC61380

11:20 — TEC61380

4:30 — TEC61380

9:35 — TEC61380

6:40 — TEC61380

3:45 — TEC61380

A Busy Day

Write the time shown on each clock.

A.

____:____ PM

B.

____:____ AM

C.

____:____ AM

D.

____:____ PM

E.

____:____ AM

F.

____:____ AM

G.

____:____ PM

H.

____:____ PM

I.

____:____ PM

J.

____:____ AM

Bonus: What might Chet do after brushing his teeth but before meeting Corky at the park? Write an event and the time to the nearest five minutes.

Order these events 1–5.

Events (AM)

____ Chet meets Corky at the park at 10:20.

____ Chet eats pancakes at 8:25.

____ Chet plays ball until 11:45.

____ Chet wakes up at 8:10.

____ Chet brushes his teeth at 8:40.

Order these events 6–10.

Events (PM)

____ Chet gets ready for bed around 7:50.

____ Chet goes on a picnic at 12:20.

____ Chet eats dinner at 6:05.

____ Chet goes fishing until 4:10.

____ Chet buys an ice cream at 1:45.

Time

Group Work

● Display the two word problem starters. Have each child choose a starter and use it to write an elapsed-time problem on the front of an index card and the solution on the back. Direct each student to exchange her card with another child. Allow time for students to solve and check their problems.

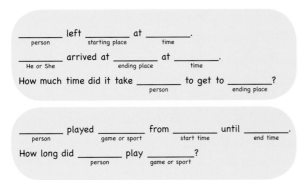

_____ left _____ at _____.
person · starting place · time

_____ arrived at _____ at _____.
He or She · ending place · time

How much time did it take _____ to get to _____?
person · ending place

_____ played _____ from _____ until _____.
person · game or sport · start time · end time

How long did _____ play _____?
person · game or sport

● Write on different sheets of card stock the numbers 1 through 12 and set them in a circle on the floor. Select two children to stand in the center of the circle: one student holding a short jump rope (hour hand) and the other student holding a long jump rope (minute hand). Place another child at the opposite end of each jump rope. Guide each pair of students to stretch the ropes and stand in the 10:15 position. Invite two students to stand outside the clock to mark the hour and minute starting time. Then instruct the students manipulating the minute hand to walk clockwise around the inside of the circle to show the passing of 20 minutes and call out the end time. Confirm the answer and then have four different students take over the clock hands.

Centers

● Write ten elapsed-time word problems and label each problem with a letter "A" through "J". Set out student copies of the clock cards from the top of page 68 and green and red colored pencils. A student selects a word problem and uses the green pencil to draw the start time on a clock card and the red pencil to draw the end time. She writes on her paper the letter of the word problem; glues the clock next to the letter; and writes the start, end, and elapsed times.

A
start time 6:30
end time 7:15
elapsed time 45 minutes

● Provide a copy of the spinner pattern from page 68 and a paper clip. A student divides and labels a sheet of paper as shown. He spins the spinner one time and copies the time in the first column. He spins the spinner a second time and copies the elapsed time in the second column. Then the child determines the end time and writes his answer in the third column. He continues the activity seven or more times.

Start time	End time	Elapsed time
3:22	1 hour, 40 minutes	5:02

Seatwork See page 69.

Clock Cards

Use with the first center activity on page 67.

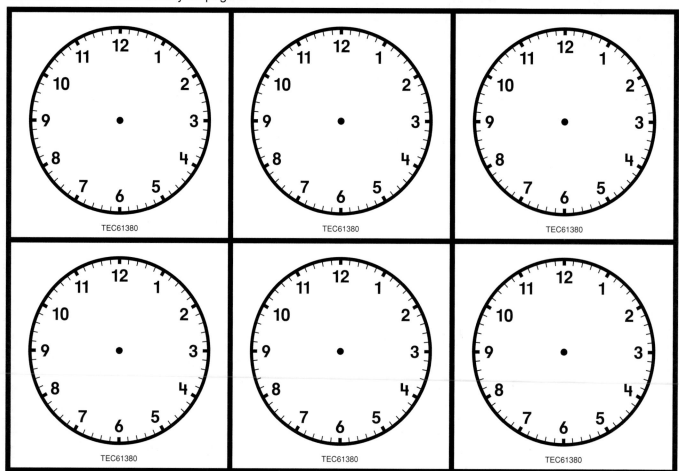

TEC61380   TEC61380   TEC61380

TEC61380   TEC61380   TEC61380

Spinner Pattern

Use with the second center activity on page 67.

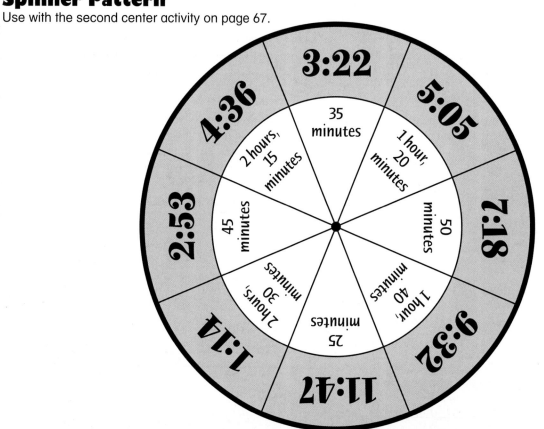

Name_____

Time to Bake

Solve.
Cut apart the clocks below.
Glue each clock next to its matching digital time.

A. Hilda wakes up at 4:45 AM. She leaves her house 36 minutes
   later. What time does Hilda leave her house?

   _____ : _____ AM

B. Hilda leaves her driveway at 5:23 AM. She gets to the bakery 21
   minutes later. What time does Hilda arrive at the bakery?

   _____ : _____ AM

C. Muffins take 15 minutes to bake. Hilda takes the first batch of
   muffins out of the oven at 6:10 AM. What time did Hilda put the
   muffins in the oven?

   _____ : _____ AM

D. Hilda puts a cake in the oven at 8:37 AM. The cake takes 1 hour
   and 16 minutes to bake. What time is the cake done?

   _____ : _____ AM

E. The last batch of cookies takes 36 minutes to bake. Hilda takes
   the cookies out of the oven at 2:54 PM. What time did Hilda put
   the cookies in the oven?

   _____ : _____ PM

F. It takes Hilda 47 minutes to clean the kitchen. She starts
   cleaning at 3:20 PM. What time does Hilda finish cleaning the
   kitchen?

   _____ : _____ PM

Bonus: Look at the answers to problems B and F. Use the times to figure out the number
of hours and minutes Hilda spends at the bakery.

Quick Plans: Math • ©The Mailbox® Books • TEC61380 • Key p. 96

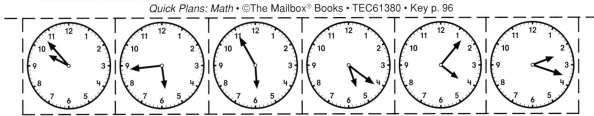

Money

Group Work

● Put in resealable bags different coin combinations such as quarters, nickels, and pennies and dimes, nickels, and pennies. Write on the board a value between 25 cents and 99 cents. Give each group a bag and have students model the value with their coins. Instruct one student from each group to draw on the board the coins that match her group's model. Then repeat the activity with another value.

● Make student copies of page 71 and display the coin code shown. Form groups of four and give each group a set of money manipulatives and a die. Have each student take a turn rolling the die and placing the matching coin or dollar bill on his mat. If a child can, he trades coin sets of equal values to have the least number of coins on his mat. The game is over once a child collects five dollars.

Coin Code
1 = penny
2 = nickel
3 = dime
4 = quarter
5 or 6 = dollar

Centers

● Fill a resealable bag with coins that total 99 cents. Gather small decorative items—such as stickers, paper cutouts, chenille stems, wiggle eyes, buttons, and ribbons—and label each item with a price between one cent and 99 cents. Also provide a supply of construction paper. A student uses the coins to buy decorative items to use to design a picture, paying for an item before adding it to her picture. When the child finishes her picture, she writes on the back of her paper her name and the amount of money she spent.

● Program index cards with different coin values less than one dollar. Also set out coin rubber stampers and colored pencils. A student selects a card and uses the coin stampers to show a combination of coins that equal the value written on the card, stamping the coins horizontally in the form of a caterpillar. Next the child draws details such as antennae and legs. Then he writes an equal sign and the value of the coins.

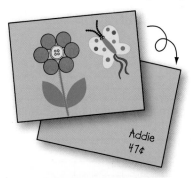

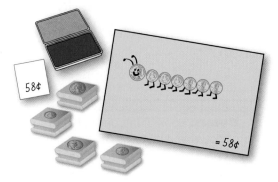

Seatwork See page 72.

pennies	nickels	dimes	quarters	dollars

Note to the teacher: Use with the second group activity on page 70.

Easy Money

Solve.
Show your work using pictures, numbers, or words.

---

1. Frisky has 1 quarter, 2 nickels, and 8 pennies. Scamper has 2 dimes, 1 nickel, and 6 pennies. How much money do the squirrels have in all?

_____ ¢

2. Frisky finds 5 nickels under a park bench. Scamper finds 1 dime and 2 pennies near the trash can. Which squirrel found the greater value of coins? How do you know?

---

3. Scamper's mom gives him 2 quarters and 3 nickels. His dad gives him 2 dimes and 5 pennies. How much money does Scamper get from his mom and dad?

_____ ¢

4. Frisky hides 1 quarter in a tree stump and 4 dimes under a rock. He buries 3 nickels and 9 pennies under an oak tree. How much money does Frisky hide?

_____ ¢

---

5. Scamper sells acorns. On Monday, he earns 4 dollars. On Tuesday, he earns 8 dollars. How much money does Scamper earn in two days?

$_____

6. Frisky borrows 1 quarter and 4 nickels from Scamper on Wednesday. He borrows 5 dimes and 3 pennies on Thursday. How much money does Frisky borrow from Scamper?

_____ ¢

---

7. Scamper has saved $23.00. If he has only one- and five-dollar bills, what are two different combinations of dollar bills Scamper can have?

8. Frisky has 3 ten-dollar bills, 4 five-dollar bills, and 8 one-dollar bills. He wants to buy a scooter that costs $48.00. Does he have enough money? How do you know?

Bonus: Scamper empties his bank. There are 12 coins in his bank. The total of the coins is 66¢. What coins are in Scamper's bank?

Line Plots

Group Work

- Draw a line plot on the board and label it in inches from 5 to 10. Have each student use a ruler to measure the length of her foot to the nearest inch and then mark the data on the line plot. Next, draw another line plot and label it in quarter inches from 5 to 10. Direct each student to measure her foot a second time to the nearest quarter inch and mark the results on the line plot. Compare and discuss the data between the two line plots.

- Direct each child to measure the length of one of his pencils from the tip to the top of the eraser and record the measurement on a sticky note. Draw a line plot on the board and label the horizontal axis in half-inch intervals from 2 to 7. Guide each student to place his sticky note on the line plot. Use the line plot data to lead a class discussion.

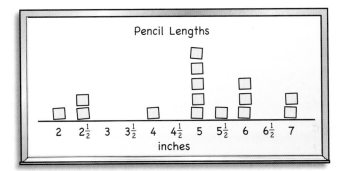

Centers

- *Partner Game:* Cut drinking straws into lengths of 3 inches, 3¼ inches, 3½ inches, 3¾ inches, and 4 inches so that there are a varying amount of each size but a total of 12 pieces. Put the pieces in a paper bag. Also set out red and blue colored pencils and a ruler. One child draws a line plot with the lengths shown; then each player selects a colored pencil. Player 1 draws a straw from the bag, estimates its length, and then measures the straw. If her estimate is correct, she marks an X on the line plot and sets the straw aside. If her estimate is incorrect, she returns the straw to the bag. Players take turns in this manner until all the straws are plotted on the line plot. The player with more Xs wins!

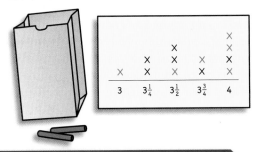

- Set out a ruler, a copy of the caterpillar cards on page 74; and student copies of the recording sheet from the same page. A student selects a card, measures the length of the caterpillar to the nearest centimeter, and marks the corresponding row of the tally chart. She repeats the steps until all the caterpillars are measured. Then she uses the data on the tally chart to make a line plot of the caterpillar lengths and writes one statement about the data results.

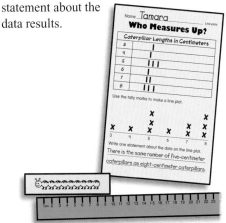

Seatwork See page 75.

Caterpillar Cards and Recording Sheet

Use with the second center activity on page 73.

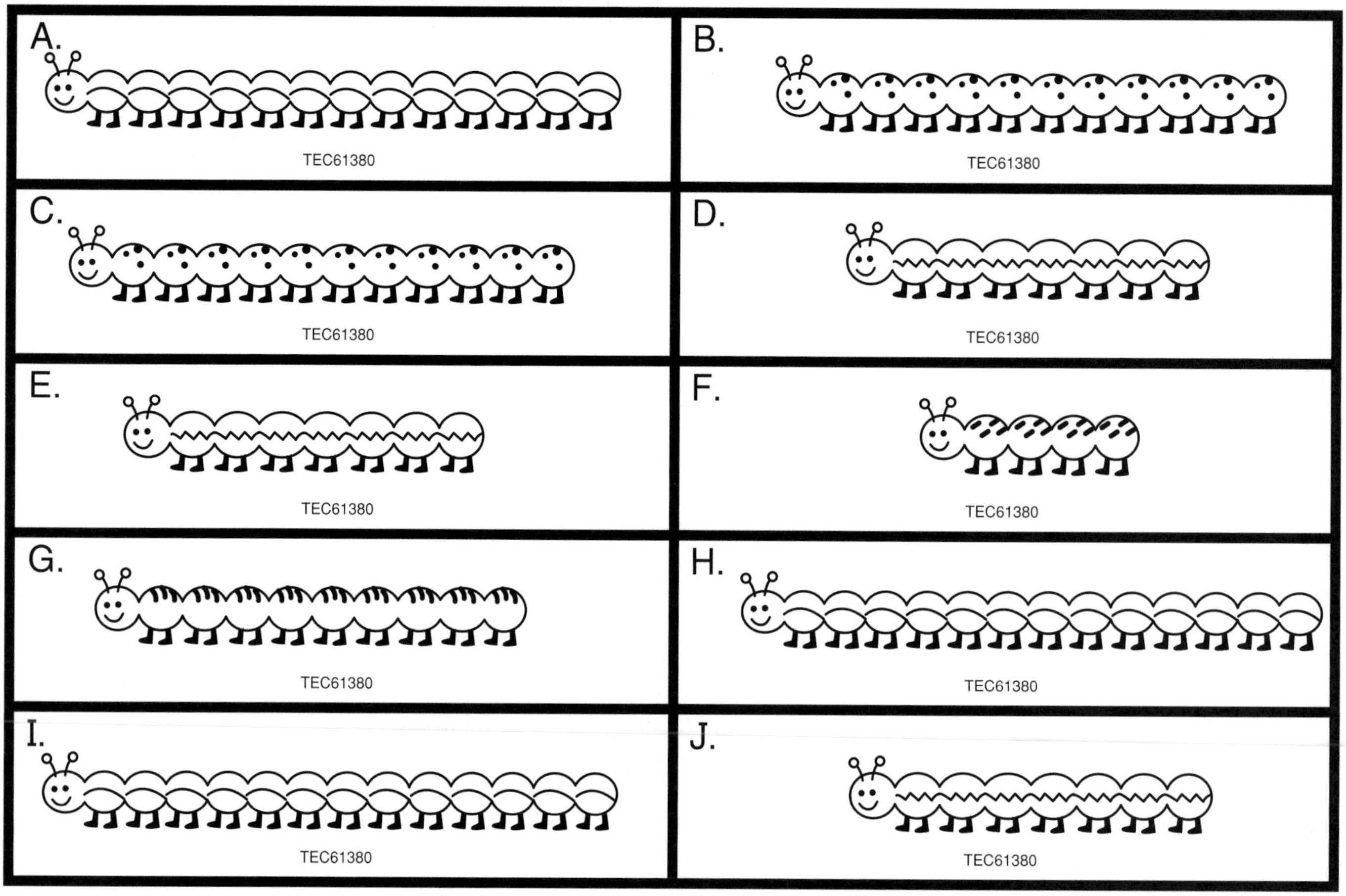

A.	B.
TEC61380	TEC61380
C.	D.
TEC61380	TEC61380
E.	F.
TEC61380	TEC61380
G.	H.
TEC61380	TEC61380
I.	J.
TEC61380	TEC61380

Line plots

Who Measures Up?

Caterpillar Lengths in Centimeters

3	
4	
5	
6	
7	
8	

Use the tally marks to make a line plot.

3 cm 4 cm 5 cm 6 cm 7 cm 8 cm

Write one statement about the data on the line plot.

_____

74

Quick Plans: Math • ©The Mailbox® Books • TEC61380 • Key p. 96

Great Lengths

Measure the length of each trail to the nearest centimeter.

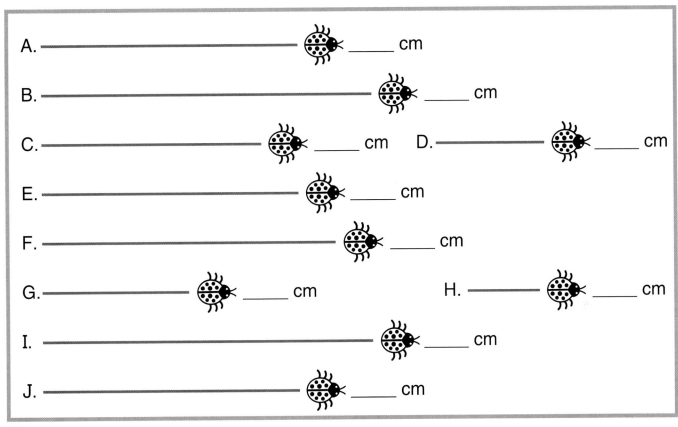

A. _____ _____ cm

B. _____ _____ cm

C. _____ _____ cm   D. _____ _____ cm

E. _____ _____ cm

F. _____ _____ cm

G. _____ _____ cm   H. _____ _____ cm

I. _____ _____ cm

J. _____ _____ cm

Draw an X to show each measurement on the line plot.

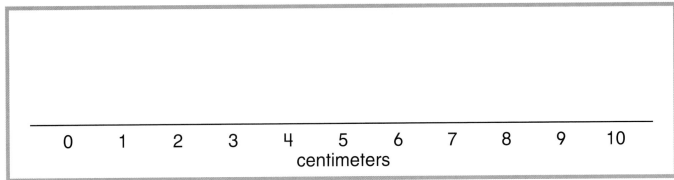

```
    0    1    2    3    4    5    6    7    8    9    10
                        centimeters
```

Write two statements about the line plot.

_____

_____

_____

_____

Bonus: Write a definition for *line plot*.

Picture and Bar Graphs

Group Work

● Draw on the board a bar graph labeled with four different lunch items. Give each student a paper circle and direct her to draw on it one of the lunch items. In turn, invite each child to tape her plate with the matching lunch item on the graph. When all the plates are in place, have each student use the data to make a bar graph on a sheet of paper. Then instruct her to write three questions and answers about the graph.

● Gather different sets of seasonal stickers to use with specific survey questions, such as fall leaves for "What is your favorite fall activity?" and snowflakes for "What do you like about snow?" Write each question on chart paper and draw a graph under each question. Display the charts around the room and tape a sheet of stickers next to each graph. Have each child use one sticker to record his response on each graph. When the graphs are completed, give one to each small group of students and instruct them to write five statements about the graph.

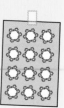

What do you like to do with snow?
make snow forts
build snowmen
sled
ski
go snow-tubing

Centers

● Set out a supply of store circulars and a supply of graph paper. A student sorts through a circular to gather information about kinds of items represented. She makes a tally chart of the data and then uses it to make a bar graph. The child tallies her graph and writes three statements about the results.

● Cut apart a card stock copy of the animal cracker cards from page 77 and store the cards in a small bowl. Also set out student copies of the recording sheet from the same page. A student sorts the cards and records on the tally chart the total number of each animal cracker. He uses the tally marks to complete the graph; then he writes on his paper a question and answer about the graph.

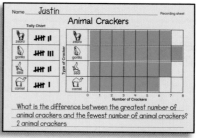

Seatwork See page 78.

Use with the second center activity on page 76.

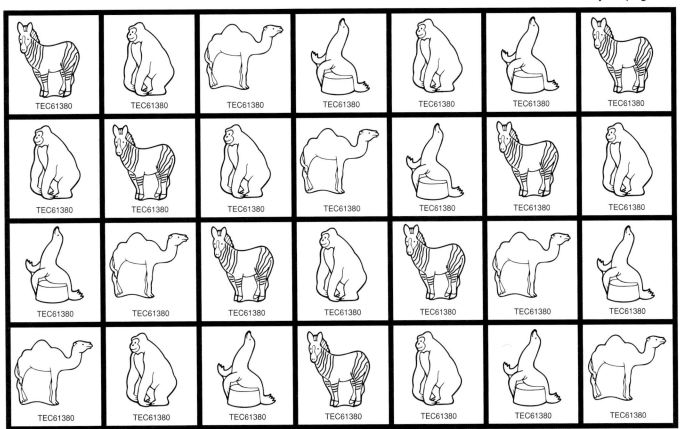

Name _____ Recording sheet

Animal Crackers

Tally Chart

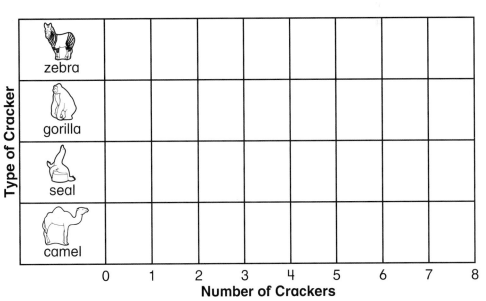

Type of Cracker: zebra, gorilla, seal, camel

Number of Crackers: 0 1 2 3 4 5 6 7 8

Yori's Yummy Yogurt Bar

Read the clues to make a bar graph.

1. Twelve yogurts with jelly beans were sold.	2. The number of yogurts with peanuts was 4 less than the number of yogurts with jelly beans.	3. Twice as many yogurts with raisins than peanuts were sold.
4. Eighteen yogurts with dried berries sold before lunch. After lunch, 11 more yogurts with dried berries were sold.	5. Nine more yogurts with chocolate chips were sold than yogurts with jelly beans.	6. The number of yogurts with coconut was 8 less than the number of yogurts with raisins.

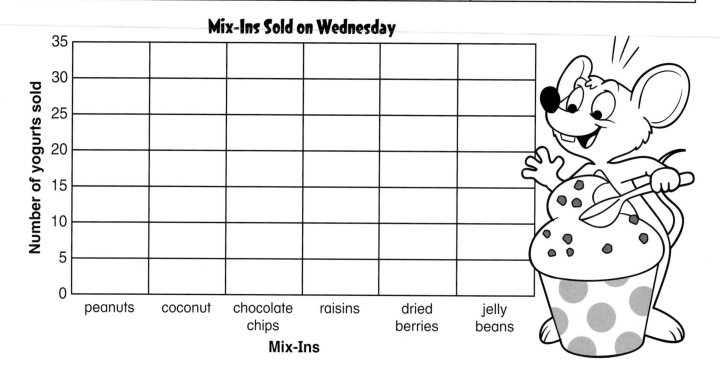

Mix-Ins Sold on Wednesday

Number of yogurts sold (y-axis: 0, 5, 10, 15, 20, 25, 30, 35)

x-axis: peanuts, coconut, chocolate chips, raisins, dried berries, jelly beans

Mix-Ins

7. How many yogurts in all were sold? _____ yogurts

8. How many more yogurts with dried berries sold than jelly bean yogurts?

_____ more dried berries

Bonus: If 2 more yogurts with each mix-in were sold, how many of each mix-in was sold on Wednesday?

peanuts _____   coconut _____   chocolate chips _____

raisins _____   dried berries _____   jelly beans _____

Area

Group Work

● For each group, cut out a different-size construction paper square, such as 3" x 3", 6" x 6", or 12" x 12". Then use masking tape to mark off various rectangles on the floor, such as 1' x 3', 2' x 4', and 3' x 5'. Label each rectangle with a letter. Give each group a paper square and have them rotate from rectangle to rectangle to measure and record the area of each one.

● Give each student a two-inch, three-inch, and four-inch paper square and 16 square crackers. Have each child cover the smallest paper square with a layer of crackers and then count the crackers to determine the area in square units. Ask students to name two of the side lengths and write a multiplication sentence to solve for the area. Then repeat the activity with the remaining paper squares. Invite students to munch on their crackers when the work is all done!

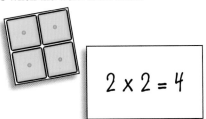

$$2 \times 2 = 4$$

Centers

● Cut and laminate several construction paper rectangles of various whole-inch lengths. Label each rectangle with a different letter. Set out the rectangles, one-inch square tiles or Unifix cubes and centimeter cubes. A student selects a rectangle, writes the letter of the rectangle on her paper, and places tiles on one horizontal and one vertical side. She multiplies the number of horizontal tiles by the number of vertical tiles and records the area of the rectangle. Then she checks her answer by covering the surface of the rectangle with tiles and counting the total number. The child repeats the activity with the same rectangle but a different unit of measurement.

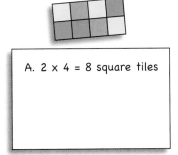

A. 2 x 4 = 8 square tiles

● Cut apart a copy of the cards on page 80 and set them out with one-inch square tiles. A student selects a card and uses the tiles to make a model of the shape or shapes as shown on the card. The child counts all the tiles to determine the total area of the shape. He writes on his paper the letter of the card and the area of the shape.

A. 9 square units
B. 8 square units
C. 15 square units
D. 26 square units
E. 33 square units
F. 23 square units
G. 30 square units
H. 15 square units
I. 16 square units

Seatwork See page 81.

Area Cards

Use with the second center activity on page 79.

Ⓐ What is the area?

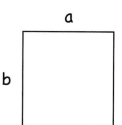

a = 3 units
b = 3 units

TEC61380

Ⓑ What is the area?

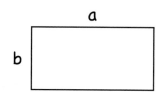

a = 4 units
b = 2 units

TEC61380

Ⓒ What is the area?

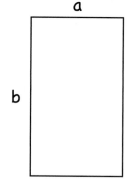

a = 3 units
b = 5 units

TEC61380

Ⓓ What is the area?

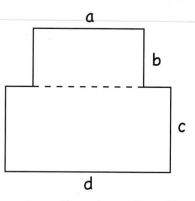

a = 4 units   b = 2 units
c = 3 units   d = 6 units

TEC61380

Ⓔ What is the area?

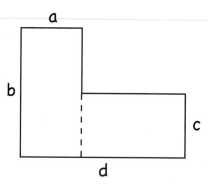

a = 3 units   b = 6 units
c = 3 units   d = 5 units

TEC61380

Ⓕ What is the area?

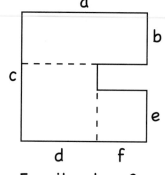

a = 5 units   b = 2 units
c = 5 units   d = 3 units
e = 2 units   f = 2 units

TEC61380

Ⓖ What is the area?

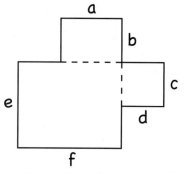

a = 3 units   b = 2 units
c = 2 units   d = 2 units
e = 4 units   f = 5 units

TEC61380

Ⓗ What is the area?

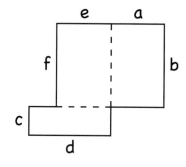

a = 2 units   b = 3 units
c = 1 unit   d = 3 units
e = 2 units   f = 3 units

TEC61380

Ⓘ What is the area?

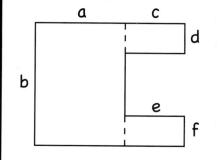

a = 3 units   b = 4 units
c = 2 units   d = 1 unit
e = 2 units   f = 1 unit

TEC61380

Quick Plans: Math •©The Mailbox® Books • TEC61380

What a Water Park!

Look at the map.

Boys' Lockers

Fish Pond

Rowboats

Waterfall Ridge

Girls' Lockers

Splash Fountain

Diving Pool

Wave Pool

Snack Bar

Slippery Slide

☐ = 1 square foot

Complete the chart.

Section	Side Lengths		Area
A. Waterfall Ridge	8 sq. ft.	6 sq. ft.	48 sq. ft.
B. Wave Pool			
C. Boys' Lockers			
D. Girls' Lockers			
E. Snack Bar			
F. Fish Pond			
G. Rowboats			
H. Splash Fountain			
I. Diving Pool			
J. Slippery Slide			

To find the area of a rectangle, multiply the side lengths.

Bonus: What is the definition of *area*?

Perimeter

Group Work

● Give each trio of students six rectangular prisms of different sizes and a supply of Unifix cubes. Student 1 selects a prism and writes its name on a sheet of paper. Student 2 traces an outline of the prism onto the paper. Student 3 connects Unifix cubes along the four side lengths of the prism. Then Student 1 counts the number of cubes and Student 2 writes the total number of cubes (perimeter) inside the tracing. The students switch roles and repeat the activity with the remaining objects.

● Project a copy of page 83. Have students predict which shape will have the largest perimeter and which will have the smallest perimeter. Invite different students to count the squares in each side length to find the perimeter of a shape and write it near its letter. Then lead students in a discussion of the results.

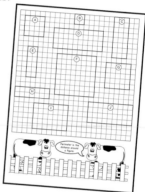

Centers

● Provide an index card labeled with names of different objects in the room, such as a bulletin board, the computer table, or the teacher's desk. A child traces his shoe and cuts it out. He selects two objects from the list and uses his cutout to measure the perimeter of each one. He writes his findings on a sheet of paper and then compares the measurements.

● Program each of ten index cards with a different number from one to ten. Also set out 40 one-inch square tiles. A student selects two cards, counts out two sets of tiles to match the numbers (side-lengths) written on the cards, and arranges the tiles to form a rectangle. She draws on her paper the rectangle, labels the side lengths, and writes the perimeter. The child repeats the activity to build three more models.

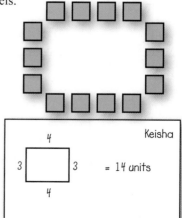

Seatwork See page 84.

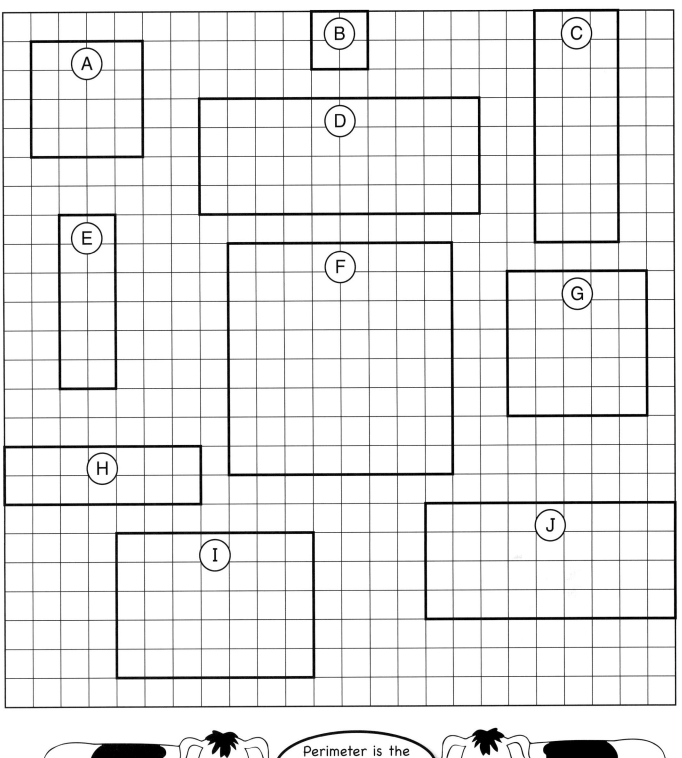

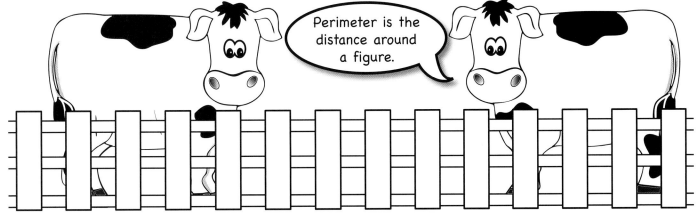

Quick Plans: Math • ©The Mailbox® Books • TEC61380 • Key p. 96

Note to the teacher: Use with the second group activity on page 82.

83

All Around the Ranch

Find the missing side length of each figure.

A.
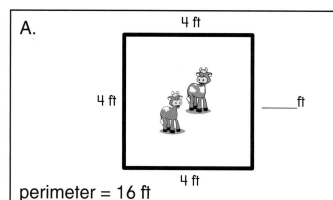
4 ft

4 ft   _____ ft

4 ft

perimeter = 16 ft

B.

_____ ft

3 ft

6 ft

perimeter = 14 ft

C.
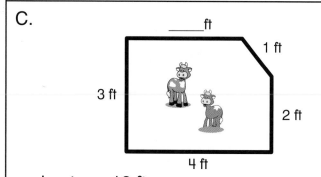
_____ ft

1 ft

3 ft

2 ft

4 ft

perimeter = 13 ft

D.
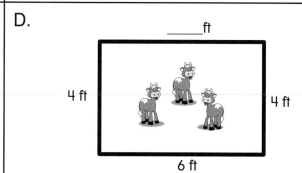
_____ ft

4 ft   4 ft

6 ft

perimeter = 20 ft

E.
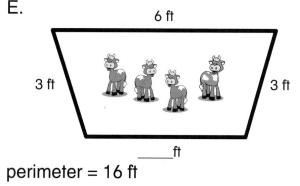
6 ft

3 ft   3 ft

_____ ft

perimeter = 16 ft

F.
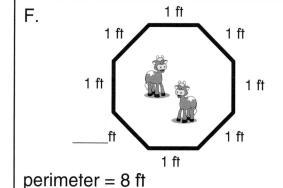
1 ft

1 ft   1 ft

1 ft   1 ft

_____ ft   1 ft

1 ft

perimeter = 8 ft

G.
4 ft

1 ft

3 ft

2 ft   3 ft

_____ ft

perimeter = 20 ft

H.
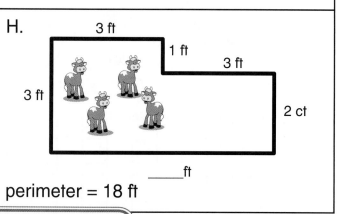
3 ft

1 ft

3 ft

3 ft

2 ct

_____ ft

perimeter = 18 ft

Bonus: What is the definition of *perimeter*?

Shapes and Attributes

Group Work

● Tape a geometric card stock shape to the back of each child's chair. To begin, play music and have students march around the classroom. Next, stop the music and direct each child to sit in the chair closest to him. Ask a question such as "Who is sitting in a chair with a square?" or "Who is sitting in a chair that has a shape with three angles?" Verify each answer; then continue as time allows.

● Give each child a supply of uncooked linguine noodles. Direct him to break some in half and break others into fourths. Call out the attributes of a specific quadrilateral and have each student construct the shape at his workspace. Then invite a volunteer to model the shape on an overhead projector or under a document camera. Continue the activity with other quadrilaterals as well as triangles, pentagons, and hexagons.

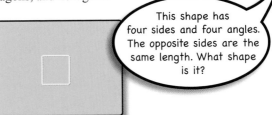

This shape has four sides and four angles. The opposite sides are the same length. What shape is it?

Centers

● *Partner Game:* Cut apart two card stock copies of the cards from page 86. Each player is dealt seven cards; then one card is laid faceup and the rest are stacked facedown. The object of the game is to make sets of four cards where each card in the set represents the same shape. To take a turn, a player takes the faceup card or the top card in the stack. If she makes a set, she lays it down and draws four more cards from the stack. To end her turn, she discards one card in the faceup pile, keeping seven cards in her hand. Play continues until no more cards can be played. The player with more sets wins.

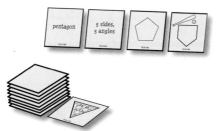

● Prepare three or more cards that each list a different combination of shapes and post the color code. Provide drawing paper, a ruler, and colored pencils. A student selects a card; then he uses the ruler and colored pencils to create a design that includes the shapes listed.

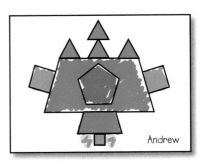

Andrew

Color Code
triangle = green
quadrilateral = blue
pentagon = red
hexagon = yellow
square = orange

Seatwork See page 87.

Shape Playing Cards

Use with the first center activity on page 85.

triangle TEC61380	3 sides, 3 angles TEC61380	 TEC61380	 TEC61380
quadrilateral TEC61380	4 sides, 4 angles TEC61380	 TEC61380	 TEC61380
pentagon TEC61380	5 sides, 5 angles TEC61380	 TEC61380	 TEC61380
hexagon TEC61380	6 sides, 6 angles TEC61380	 TEC61380	 TEC61380
cube TEC61380	6 faces, 8 vertices TEC61380	 TEC61380	 TEC61380

Coming Home

Look at the birdhouse to complete the chart.

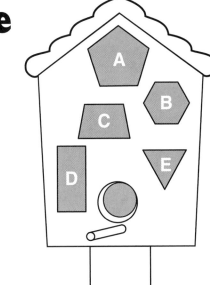

Word Bank

hexagon   pentagon   rectangle
trapezoid   triangle

	shape	number of sides	number of corners (vertices)	number of angles
A				
B				
C				
D				
E				

Write **T** for true or **F** for false.

1. _____ A shape has the same number of angles and sides.

2. _____ A trapezoid has four right angles.

3. _____ All triangles have three sides.

4. _____ All the sides of a rectangle are always the same length.

5. _____ A hexagon has more sides than a pentagon.

Bonus: A rectangle and a trapezoid are quadrilaterals. Draw another shape that is a quadrilateral. Write the name of the shape and the number of its sides, vertices, and angles.

Shapes and Attributes

Group Work

- Cut apart a copy of the question cards on page 89. Form teams and give each team a two- or three-dimensional object or a picture of one. Read a card aloud and have each team answer the question based on its shape. If a team correctly answers the question, it earns two points, unless it answers a question with a number, in which case it earns the matching number of points. If a team's answer is incorrect, it does not earn any points. The team with the most points wins!

- Direct each student to fold opposite ends of a sheet of paper an equal distance toward the center and then fold the paper in half. Have her unfold the paper one time and cut the two remaining flaps to make four flaps. Instruct the child to lift up all the flaps and draw a quadrilateral. Then have her close the flaps and write on each one a different attribute clue related to the quadrilateral.

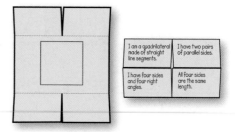

Centers

- Place inside six paper bags a different combination of three or four pattern blocks; then label the bags A–F. A student selects a bag, writes the letter of the bag on his paper, and removes the blocks from the bag. Then he constructs one of four quadrilaterals—a square, rectangle, trapezoid, or parallelogram—with the blocks. He writes the name of the quadrilateral he made and traces the shapes on his paper. The child returns the blocks to the bag and selects another bag.

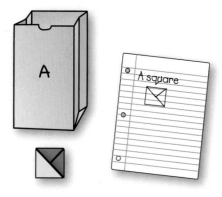

- Set out a supply of drawing paper and colored pencils. A student labels a sheet of paper with the question shown. On the left side of the paper, she draws a frame with a quadrilateral of her choice inside it. Under the drawing, she lists the shape's name, attributes, and places where she has seen examples of the shape. The child repeats the activity with a different shape on the right side of the paper. After both drawings are complete, she writes across the bottom of her paper the message shown and signs her name.

Seatwork See page 90.

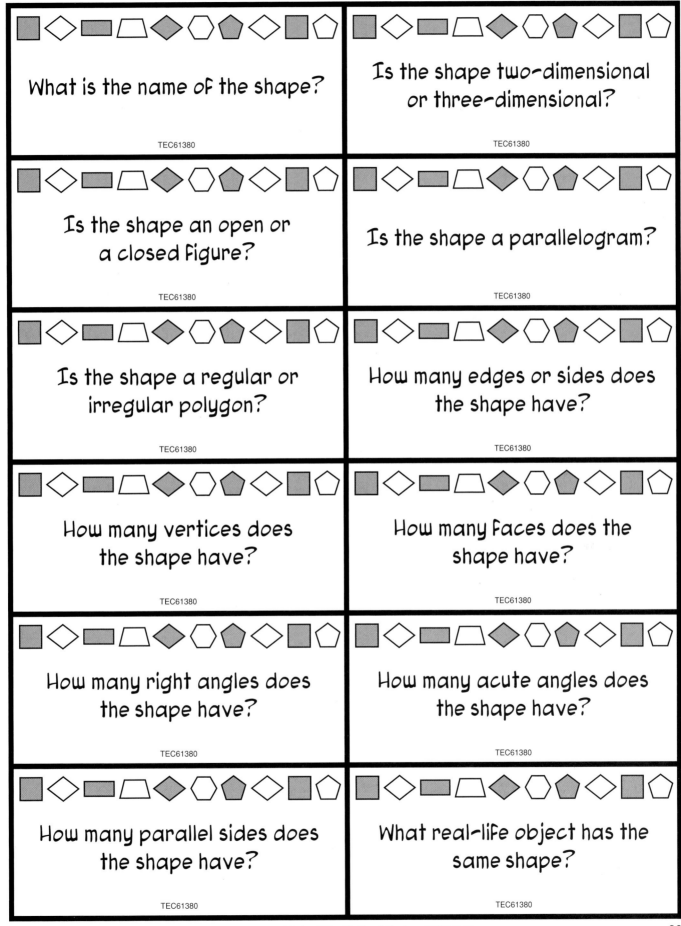

What is the name of the shape?

TEC61380

Is the shape two-dimensional or three-dimensional?

TEC61380

Is the shape an open or a closed figure?

TEC61380

Is the shape a parallelogram?

TEC61380

Is the shape a regular or irregular polygon?

TEC61380

How many edges or sides does the shape have?

TEC61380

How many vertices does the shape have?

TEC61380

How many faces does the shape have?

TEC61380

How many right angles does the shape have?

TEC61380

How many acute angles does the shape have?

TEC61380

How many parallel sides does the shape have?

TEC61380

What real-life object has the same shape?

TEC61380

Moving Day

Cross off the shape that does not belong in each set.

Write a reason why the shape does not belong.

Use the word bank to help.

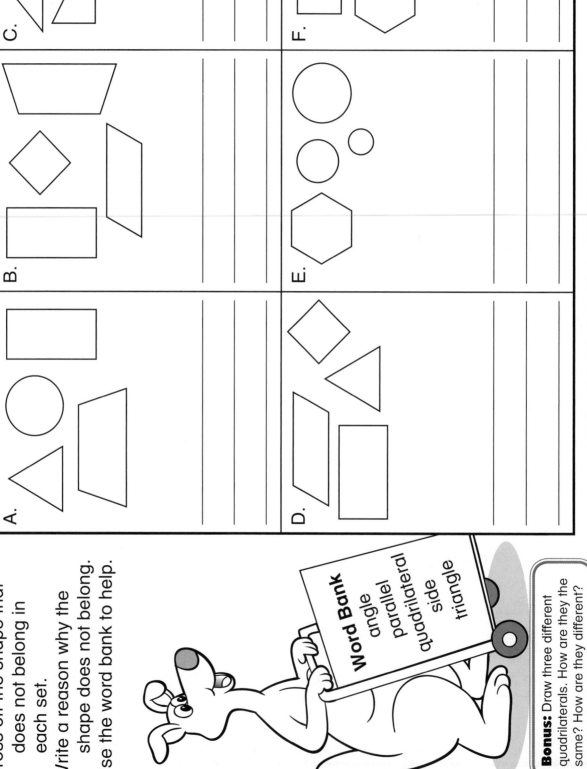

Word Bank
angle
parallel
quadrilateral
side
triangle

Bonus: Draw three different quadrilaterals. How are they the same? How are they different?

Forming and Naming Equal Shares

Group Work

● Provide each group with eight paper rectangles of the same size. Challenge each group to show all the different ways a rectangle can be folded to show halves, thirds, or fourths. Have the students label each fractional part as halves, thirds, or fourths.

● Form two groups and assign one group circles and the other rectangles. Announce a term, such as two halves or one-third. Select one member from each team to go to the board and draw a picture of his team's shape, partitioning and shading it to match the term. Leave the shape on the board, and repeat the activity with a different term. As terms are repeated, challenge students to show a different representation of those terms.

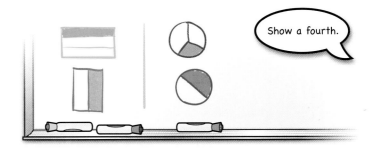

Show a fourth.

Centers

● *Partner Game:* Cut apart a copy of the game cards at the top of page 92. To prepare, each student draws a 3 x 3 grid and programs each space with a unit fraction with the denominators 2, 3, 4, 6, and 8. (Some fractions will be repeated.) To play, Player 1 shuffles the game cards and stacks them facedown. Player 2 flips the top card over. Each player crosses off a matching fraction on his grid. If a player does not have a matching fraction or it has already been marked, he does nothing to his grid. Then Player 1 draws the next card. Players alternate turns until one child crosses off three fractions in a row horizontally, vertically, or diagonally.

● Put a copy of the cards from the bottom of page 92 in an envelope. Also provide a set of pattern blocks. A student reads a card and gathers the matching pattern blocks. She pieces the blocks together to make a whole shape. Then the child traces the shape onto her paper as shown, labels each fraction, and writes the name of the whole shape.

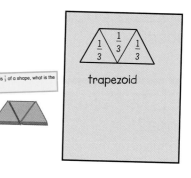

A. If a △ is ⅓ of a shape, what is the shape?

trapezoid

Seatwork See page 93.

Game Cards

Use with the first center activity on page 91.

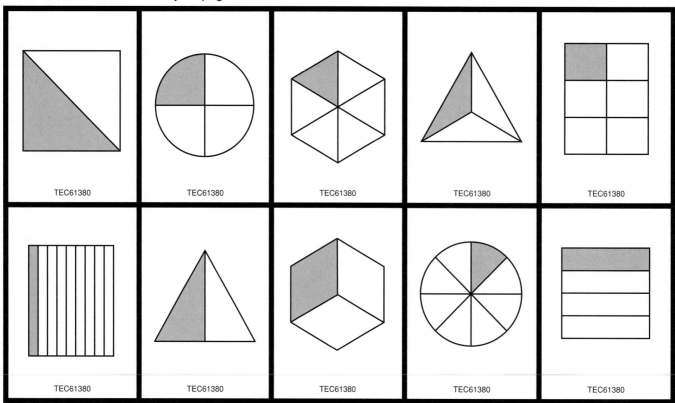

Activity Cards

Use with the second center activity on page 91.

A. If a ▽ is $\frac{1}{3}$ of a shape, what is the shape? TEC61380	B. If a ▽ is $\frac{1}{6}$ of a shape, what is the shape? TEC61380
C. If a ▱ is $\frac{1}{3}$ of a shape, what is the shape? TEC61380	D. If a ▱ is $\frac{1}{4}$ of a shape, what is the shape? TEC61380
E. If a ⬓ is $\frac{1}{2}$ of a shape, what is the shape? TEC61380	F. If a ◺ is $\frac{1}{8}$ of a shape, what is the shape? TEC61380
G. If a ☐ is $\frac{1}{3}$ of a shape, what is the shape? TEC61380	H. If a ☐ is $\frac{1}{4}$ of a shape, what is the shape? TEC61380
I. If a ◇ is $\frac{1}{2}$ of a shape, what is the shape? TEC61380	J. If a ◇ is $\frac{1}{4}$ of a shape, what is the shape? TEC61380

Sweet Shares

Follow the directions.
Color one part of the divided shape.
Write the fraction for the colored part.

Divide into 4 equal parts.	Divide into 2 equal parts.	Divide into 3 equal parts.
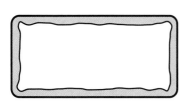 _____	 _____	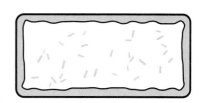 _____
Divide into 2 equal parts.	Divide into 8 equal parts.	Divide into 2 equal parts.
 _____	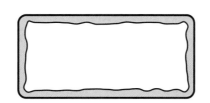 _____	 _____
Divide into 3 equal parts.	Divide into 6 equal parts.	Divide into 4 equal parts.
 _____	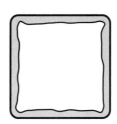 _____	 _____
Divide into 4 equal parts.	Divide into 8 equal parts.	Divide into 6 equal parts.
 _____	 _____	 _____

Bonus: Draw 3 squares. Show 3 different ways to divide a square into 4 equal parts.

Answer Keys

Page 6

A. 7	N. 8
B. 3	O. 11
C. 8	P. 7
D. 10	Q. 13
E. 13	R. 6
F. 9	S. 4
G. 7	T. 6
H. 4	U. 7
I. 15	V. 13
J. 10	W. 8
K. 9	X. 5
L. 2	Y. 12
M. 6	Z. 5

Bonus: Order will vary; 6 + 4 = 10 or
4 + 6 = 10, 6 − 4 = 2

Page 9

A. 50	D. 81
B. 55	E. 38
C. 90	F. 23

Bonus: Answers will vary.

Page 12

A. 2 + 2 + 2 + 2 + 2 + 2 = 12
B. 3 + 3 + 3 = 9
C. 2 + 2 + 2 + 2 + 2 = 10
D. 7 + 7 + 7 = 21
E. 6 + 6 + 6 + 6 = 24
F. 4 + 4 + 4 + 4 + 4 + 4 + 4 = 28
G. 3 + 3 + 3 + 3 + 3 + 3 = 18
H. 8 + 8 = 16
I. 5 + 5 + 5 + 5 + 5 + 5 = 30
J. 4 + 4 + 4 = 12
K. 3 + 3 + 3 + 3 + 3 + 3 + 3 + 3 = 24
L. 5 + 5 + 5 = 15
M. 8 + 8 + 8 = 24
N. 4 + 4 + 4 + 4 + 4 = 20
O. 1 + 1 + 1 + 1 + 1 = 5
P. 8 + 8 + 8 + 8 + 8 = 40
Q. 2 + 2 + 2 + 2 + 2 + 2 + 2 + 2 + 2 = 18
R. 5 + 5 + 5 + 5 + 5 + 5 + 5 = 35
S. 9 + 9 + 9 + 9 + 9 + 9 = 54
T. 7 + 7 + 7 + 7 + 7 + 7 + 7 = 49

Bonus: 3 x 9 = 27 or 9 x 3 = 27,
3 + 3 + 3 + 3 + 3 + 3 + 3 + 3 + 3 = 27, 9 + 9 + 9 = 27

Page 15

A. 5	G. 3
B. 2	H. 1
C. 1	I. 6
D. 4	J. 4
E. 2	K. 6
F. 5	L. 3

Bonus: 16 ÷ 8 = 2 or 16 ÷ 2 = 8

Page 18

A. 18	D. 8
B. 4	E. 3
C. 24	F. 5

Bonus: Answers will vary.

Page 21

A. 9, 18 ÷ 9 = 2 or 18 ÷ 2 = 9
B. 5, 20 ÷ 5 = 4 or 20 ÷ 4 = 5
C. 7, 35 ÷ 7 = 5 or 35 ÷ 5 = 7
D. 4, 24 ÷ 4 = 6 or 24 ÷ 6 = 4
E. 3, 21 ÷ 7 = 3 or 21 ÷ 3 = 7
F. 3, 6 ÷ 3 = 2 or 6 ÷ 2 = 3
G. 7, 56 ÷ 8 = 7 or 56 ÷ 7 = 8
H. 4, 36 ÷ 4 = 9 or 36 ÷ 9 = 4
I. 4, 16 ÷ 4 = 4
J. 6, 48 ÷ 8 = 6 or 48 ÷ 6 = 8
K. 9, 54 ÷ 6 = 9 or 54 ÷ 9 = 6
L. 5, 15 ÷ 3 = 5 or 15 ÷ 5 = 3
M. 7, 14 ÷ 7 = 2 or 14 ÷ 2 = 7
N. 5, 25 ÷ 5 = 5
O. 3, 24 ÷ 8 = 3 or 24 ÷ 3 = 8
P. 6, 36 ÷ 6 = 6
Q. 8, 72 ÷ 8 = 9 or 72 ÷ 9 = 8
R. 6, 30 ÷ 5 = 6 or 30 ÷ 6 = 5
S. 7, 28 ÷ 7 = 4 or 28 ÷ 4 = 7
T. 6, 42 ÷ 7 = 6 or 42 ÷ 6 = 7

Bonus: Answers will vary.

Page 24

A. 6 x 1 = 6, 1 x 6 = 6
B. 8 x 3 = 24, 3 x 8 = 24
C. 7 x 5 = 35, 5 x 7 = 35
D. 9 x 2 = 18, 2 x 9 = 18
E. 7 x 4 = 28, 4 x 7 = 28
F. 6 x 3 = 18, 3 x 6 = 18
G. 8 x 5 = 40, 5 x 8 = 40
H. 6 x 4 = 24, 4 x 6 = 24
I. 7 x 3 = 21, 3 x 7 = 21
J. 6 x 9 = 54, 9 x 6 = 54
K. 7 x 8 = 56, 8 x 7 = 56
L. 8 x 6 = 48, 6 x 8 = 48
M. 7 x 6 = 42, 6 x 7 = 42
N. 9 x 8 = 72, 8 x 9 = 72
O. 7 x 9 = 63, 9 x 7 = 63

Bonus: 5 x 6 = 30, 6 x 8 = 48, 2 x 7 = 14

Page 26

Order of factors will vary.
APE, (2 x 7) x 3 = 42; CAR, (2 x 2) x 7 = 28;
DAD, (2 x 3) x 3 = 18; EAR, (3 x 2) x 7 = 42;
HAT, (4 x 2) x 8 = 64, LIP, (5 x 4) x 7 = 140;
MAD, (3 x 2) x 6 = 36; YAK, (9 x 2) x 5 = 90

Page 27

(3 x 2) x 4 =	8 x (2 x 5) =	6 x (4 x 2) =
3 x 2 = 6	2 x 5 = 10	4 x 2 = 8
6 x 4 = 24	10 x 8 = 80	8 x 6 = 48
3 x (2 x 4) = 24 Ⓒ	(8 x 2) x 5 = 80 Ⓖ	(6 x 4) x 2 = 48 Ⓢ
(4 x 5) x 3 =	(5 x 6) x 9 =	(2 x 4) x 8 =
4 x 5 = 20	5 x 6 = 30	2 x 4 = 8
20 x 3 = 60	30 x 9 = 270	8 x 8 = 64
4 x (5 x 3) = 60 Ⓔ	5 x (6 x 9) = 270 Ⓣ	2 x (4 x 8) = 64 Ⓐ
(2 x 5) x 9 =	(5 x 6) x 7 =	6 x (3 x 2) =
2 x 5 = 10	5 x 6 = 30	3 x 2 = 6
10 x 9 = 90	30 x 7 = 210	6 x 6 = 36
2 x (5 x 9) = 90 Ⓝ	5 x (6 x 7) = 210 Ⓗ	(6 x 3) x 2 = 36 Ⓘ
9 x (3 x 3) =	7 x (5 x 8) =	
3 x 3 = 9	5 x 8 = 40	
9 x 9 = 81	40 x 7 = 280	
(9 x 3) x 3 = 81 Ⓟ	(7 x 5) x 8 = 280 Ⓦ	

Because <u>HE WAS SITTING ON THE DECK</u>!

Bonus: Possible answers include the
following: 5 x 4 = 20, 20 x 6 = 120; 5 x 6 = 30,
30 x 4 = 120.

Page 29

☆(4 x 1) + (4 x 9), ▢(5 x 3) + (5 x 4),
⬤(3 x 1) + (3 x 10), △(2 x 1) + (2 x 7),
♥(4 x 2) + (4 x 4), ✿(5 x 1) + (5 x 7),
◇(3 x 3) + (3 x 3), ⬠(6 x 7) + (6 x 1),
☾(8 x 1) + (8 x 9)

Page 30

Ⓐ 4 x 9 = 36		Ⓑ (2 x 4) + (2 x 3)	
Ⓑ 2 x 7 = 14		Ⓓ (5 x 1) + (5 x 5)	
Ⓒ 3 x 9 = 27		Ⓞ (3 x 4) + (3 x 2)	
Ⓓ 5 x 6 = 30		Ⓘ (2 x 2) + (2 x 6)	
Ⓔ 3 x 5 = 15		Ⓕ (4 x 7) + (4 x 1)	
Ⓕ 4 x 8 = 32		Ⓛ (6 x 1) + (6 x 5)	
Ⓖ 3 x 7 = 21		Ⓗ (6 x 3) + (6 x 7)	
Ⓗ 6 x 10 = 60		Ⓚ (7 x 2) + (7 x 2)	
Ⓘ 2 x 8 = 16		Ⓐ (4 x 5) + (4 x 4)	
Ⓙ 5 x 7 = 35		Ⓖ (3 x 3) + (3 x 4)	
Ⓚ 7 x 4 = 28		Ⓜ (5 x 6) + (5 x 3)	
Ⓛ 6 x 6 = 36		Ⓝ (4 x 5) + (4 x 1)	
Ⓜ 5 x 9 = 45		Ⓟ (6 x 4) + (6 x 4)	
Ⓝ 4 x 6 = 24		Ⓔ (3 x 2) + (3 x 3)	
Ⓞ 3 x 6 = 18		Ⓙ (5 x 2) + (5 x 5)	
Ⓟ 6 x 8 = 48		Ⓒ (3 x 7) + (3 x 2)	

Bonus: Possible answers include: 3 x (1 + 7),
3 x (2 + 6), 3 x (3 + 5), 3 x (4 + 4)

Page 33

1. 10 packs
2. 3 pizzas
3. 2 cupcakes
4. 5 pieces of candy
5. 6 six-packs
6. 27 prizes

Bonus: $5

Page 36

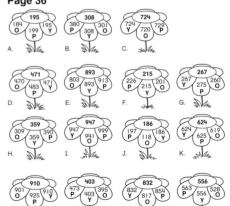

Bonus: Flowers C, E, I, K, L, N, and O should
be circled.

Page 39

23	51	89	18	61	93	36	25	45	57
20	50	(90)	(20)	60	90	(40)	(30)	(50)	(60)

965	192	784	243	435	138	857	622	361	713
(970)	190	780	240	(440)	(140)	(860)	620	360	710

645	916	452	691	142	779	324	287	828	373
600	900	(500)	(700)	100	(800)	300	(300)	800	(400)

Bonus: The first car is the winner.

Page 42
A. 72   B. 62   C. 92
D. 91   E. 41   F. 48
G. 38   H. 39   I. 79
J. 75   K. 65   L. 67

Bonus: Answers will vary.

Page 45

A 8	B 2	C 8
D 5	0	9
E 1	9	3

F 5	G 8	H 2
I 6	0	4
J 4	9	7

K 3	L 8	M 3
N 1	4	2
O 5	9	3

Bonus: Answers will vary.

Page 47
A. 200 miles   B. 80 miles
C. 140 miles   D. 360 miles
E. 180 miles   F. $120
G. 480 miles   H. 280 miles
I. 350 miles   J. 100 songs

Page 48

160 L	300 O	140 B	400 H
360 T	490 R	120 H	540 A
200 K	420 A	90 E	180 T
320 F	450 B	240 Y	630 O
150 V	640 O	80 H	210 T

THEY BOTH HAVE A LOT OF BARK.

Bonus: Answers will vary.

Page 50
2. ²⁄₆
3. ³⁄₄
4. ³⁄₆
5. ⁵⁄₆
6. ¹⁄₆
7. ⁴⁄₆
8. ³⁄₃
9. ⁰⁄₂ or 0
10. ⁵⁄₈
11. ¹⁄₈
12. ²⁄₃

Page 51
A. ³⁄₄   B. ⁴⁄₈   C. ⁷⁄₈   D. ⁶⁄₈   E. ⁴⁄₆   F. ¹⁄₃
G. ²⁄₆   H. ³⁄₈   I. ²⁄₃   J. ⁵⁄₆   K. ²⁄₄   L. ¹⁄₈

M. ¹⁄₄   ²⁄₄   ³⁄₄   ⁴⁄₄

N. ¹⁄₆   ²⁄₆   ³⁄₆   ⁴⁄₆   ⁵⁄₆   ⁶⁄₆

O. ¹⁄₈   ²⁄₈   ³⁄₈   ⁴⁄₈   ⁵⁄₈   ⁶⁄₈   ⁷⁄₈   ⁸⁄₈

Bonus: Drawings will vary.

Page 54

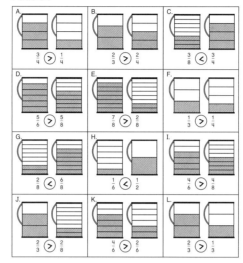

A. ³⁄₄ > ¹⁄₄   B. ²⁄₃ > ²⁄₄   C. ³⁄₈ < ³⁄₄
D. ⁵⁄₆ > ⁵⁄₈   E. ⁷⁄₈ > ²⁄₈   F. ¹⁄₃ > ¹⁄₄
G. ²⁄₈ < ⁶⁄₈   H. ¹⁄₆ < ¹⁄₂   I. ⁴⁄₆ > ⁴⁄₈
J. ²⁄₃ > ²⁄₈   K. ⁴⁄₆ > ²⁄₆   L. ²⁄₃ > ¹⁄₃

Page 57
Estimates will vary.
A 6 inches
B 3 inches
C 4½ inches
D 5½ inches
E 7 inches
F 5 inches

Bonus: Estimates will vary; 5 inches.

Page 60
A. 13 feet
B. 29 inches
C. 9 feet
D. 100 inches
E. 69 feet
F. 72 inches
G. 93 inches
H. 36 inches

Bonus: Answers will vary.

Page 62

75 liters garbage can	180 milliliters coffee cup	5 liters fishbowl	355 milliliters soda can	4 liters milk jug
480 milliliters jar	2 liters sink	15 liters large pot	37 liters fish tank	300 milliliters soup bowl
200 liters bathtub	360 milliliters water bottle	1 liter vase	240 milliliters juice box	749 liters swimming pool

Page 63

object	estimated measurement	
1. bowl of soup	(A) 300 milliliters	N. 3 liters
2. apple	(K) 180 grams	P. 18 kilograms
3 small fishbowl full of water	H. 5 milliliters	(D) 5 liters
4. textbook	C. 100 grams	(O) 1 kilogram
5. can of soda	(E) 355 milliliters	D. 3 liters
6. watermelon	L. 40 grams	(N) 4 kilograms
7. bucket of water	T. 4 milliliters	(M) 4 liters
8. television	E. 13 grams	(H) 13 kilograms
9. full kid's swimming pool	W. 750 milliliters	(L) 750 liters
10. laptop computer	N. 300 grams	(C) 3 kilograms
11. bathtub full of water	A. 15 milliliters	(Y) 150 liters
12. cell phone	(G) 140 grams	T. 4 kilograms
13. bathroom sink full of water	M. 80 milliliters	(W) 8 liters
14. golf ball	(T) 45 grams	O. 4 kilograms

HE WANTED TO MAKE A CLEAN GETAWAY!

Bonus: Answers will vary.

Page 66
A. 4:10   B. 11:45   C. 8:40   D. 1:45
E. 8:10   F. 10:20   G. 6:05   H. 7:50
I. 12:20   J. 8:25

Events (AM)

4 Chet meets Corky at the park at 10:20.
2 Chet eats pancakes at 8:25.
5 Chet plays ball until 11:45.
1 Chet wakes up at 8:10.
3 Chet brushes his teeth at 8:40.

Events (PM)

10 Chet gets ready for bed around 7:50.
6 Chet goes on a picnic at 12:20.
9 Chet eats dinner at 6:05.
8 Chet goes fishing until 4:10.
7 Chet buys an ice cream at 1:45.

Bonus: Answers will vary.

Page 69

A.	Hilda wakes up at 4:45 AM. She leaves her house 36 minutes later. What time does Hilda leave her house?	**5 : 21** AM
B.	Hilda leaves her driveway at 5:23 AM. She gets to the bakery 21 minutes later. What time does Hilda arrive at the bakery?	**5 : 44** AM
C.	Muffins take 15 minutes to bake. Hilda takes the first batch of muffins out of the oven at 6:10 AM. What time did Hilda put the muffins in the oven?	**5 : 55** AM
D.	Hilda puts a cake in the oven at 8:37 AM. The cake takes 1 hour and 16 minutes to bake. What time is the cake done?	**9 : 53** AM
E.	The last batch of cookies takes 36 minutes to bake. Hilda takes the cookies out of the oven at 2:54 PM. What time did Hilda put the cookies in the oven?	**2 : 18** PM
F.	It takes Hilda 47 minutes to clean the kitchen. She starts cleaning at 3:20 PM. What time does Hilda finish cleaning the kitchen?	**4 : 07** PM

Bonus: 10 hours and 23 minutes

Page 72

1. 74¢
2. Frisky; He has 13 cents more than Scamper.
3. 90¢
4. 89¢
5. $12.00
6. 98¢
7. Possible answers are four five-dollar and three one-dollar bills, three five-dollar and eight one-dollar bills, two five-dollar and 13 one-dollar bills, one five-dollar and 18 one-dollar bills.
8. yes; Frisky has $58.

Bonus: 1 quarter, 2 dimes, 3 nickels, and 6 pennies

Page 74

A. 8 cm
B. 7 cm
C. 7 cm
D. 5 cm
E. 5 cm
F. 3 cm
G. 6 cm
H. 8 cm
I. 8 cm
J. 5 cm

Caterpillar Lengths in Centimeters	
3	I
4	
5	III
6	I
7	II
8	III

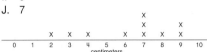

3 cm   4 cm   5 cm   6 cm   7 cm   8 cm

Page 75

A. 7
B. 9
C. 6
D. 3
E. 7
F. 8
G. 4
H. 2
I. 9
J. 7

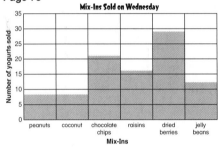

centimeters

Answers will vary.

Bonus: Definitions will vary.

Page 78

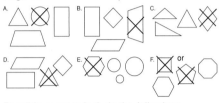

Mix-Ins Sold on Wednesday

7. 94 yogurts
8. 17 more dried berries

Bonus: peanuts 10, coconut 10, chocolate chips 23, raisins 18, dried berries 31, jelly beans 14

Page 81

A. 8 sq. ft.	6 sq. ft.	48 sq. ft.
B. 7 sq. ft.	4 sq. ft.	28 sq. ft.
C. 2 sq. ft.	3 sq. ft.	6 sq. ft.
D. 2 sq. ft.	3 sq. ft.	6 sq. ft.
E. 3 sq. ft.	4 sq. ft.	12 sq. ft.
F. 4 sq. ft.	3 sq. ft.	12 sq. ft.
G. 4 sq. ft.	2 sq. ft.	8 sq. ft.
H. 4 sq. ft.	5 sq. ft.	20 sq. ft.
I. 4 sq. ft.	6 sq. ft.	24 sq. ft.
J. 8 sq. ft.	2 sq. ft.	16 sq. ft.

Bonus: Possible definitions include *the number of square units needed to cover a plane figure.*

Page 83

A. 16 units B. 8 units C. 22 units D. 28 units
E. 16 units F. 32 units G. 20 units H. 18 units
I. 24 units J. 26 units

Page 84

A. 4 ft.
B. 5 ft.
C. 3 ft.
D. 6 ft.
E. 4 ft.
F. 1 ft.
G. 7 ft.
H. 6 ft.

Bonus: Possible definitions include *the distance around a figure.*

Page 87

	shape	number of sides	number of corners (vertices)	number of angles
A	pentagon	5	5	5
B	hexagon	6	6	6
C	trapezoid	4	4	4
D	rectangle	4	4	4
E	triangle	3	3	3

1. T
2. F
3. T
4. F
5. T

Bonus: Answers will vary but should reflect a square, rhombus, or parallelogram.

Page 90

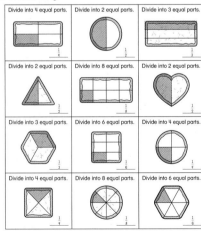

Possible reasons include the following:
A. A circle does not have sides or angles.
B. A trapezoid only has one pair of parallel sides.
C. A rhombus is not a triangle.
D. A triangle is not a quadrilateral.
E. A hexagon is not a circle.
F. A pentagon has an odd number of sides or a square is a quadrilateral.

Bonus: Answers will vary.

Page 92

A. trapezoid
B. hexagon or parallelogram
C. hexagon or parallelogram
D. rhombus or parallelogram
E. hexagon
F. hexagon
G. rectangle
H. square or rectangle
I. parallelogram
J. rhombus

Page 93

Answers will vary. Possible answers include the following:

Bonus: Drawings will vary. Possible answers include the following: